THE HOPEFUL

Copyright © 2024 by Review and Herald® Publishing Association
All rights reserved.
The Review and Herald® Publishing Association publishes biblically based materials for spiritual, physical, and mental growth and Christian discipleship.

This book was
    Edited by Penny Estes Wheeler and Rhonda J Christiano
    Copyedited by James A. Cavil
    Interior design and cover layout by Bryan Gray
    Cover image by Albert Camicioli
    Cover design by The Robot Eye
    Still Images from set by Albert Camicioli
    Photos from the Review and Herald Library

PRINTED IN U.S.A.

ISBN 978-0-8280-2914-8 (print)
        978-0-8127-6547-8 (ebook)
        978-0-8127-6548-5 (audio)

THE HOPEFUL
Hope Is on the Way

A Message From Hope Channel International

Twenty-one years ago Hope Channel International embarked on its journey with the desire to share the message of hope with as many people as possible. During the past two decades this ministry has grown to become one of the world's largest Christian media networks, with more than 80 channels worldwide, covering 100-plus languages in more than 150 countries.

Recently we created Hope Studios, a brand focused on the development and distribution of faith-based, hope-filled films. This first film, *The Hopeful*, explores the miraculous story of a group of people who were at the beginning of the tremendous spiritual movement that started with the Bible prophecies that they explored.

This Advent movement, which began more than 180 years ago, was born and gained energy from understanding prophecy, identifying a wonderful prophetic message of hope about God's love and nearness. This prophetic message transformed the perception of God from being distant and uninvolved to a God of love who is about to return and take us home. We here at Hope Channel International have taken those same biblical prophetic messages and have incorporated them into our mission and work.

Revelation 14:6 gives us the biblical prophecy that the gospel will be proclaimed to every nation, tribe, tongue, and people. In Matthew 24:14 Jesus shares that the end will come after the gospel has been preached to all the peoples of the earth. These are powerful messages that motivate us at Hope Channel!

Despite there being billions of people in the world and more than 7,000 different languages, at Hope Channel International we are both delighted and challenged by these prophecies! We long to see Jesus return soon and desire that as many people as possible hear this wonderful message of hope and are transformed by it, experiencing Jesus and His transformative love in their lives.

We are committed to employing all available resources and technologies—television, digital platforms, social media, films, etc.—to reach every audience and fulfill Bible prophecy. It inspires us to work hard and give all we can in life to fulfill these prophecies, because we eagerly anticipate Jesus' imminent return!

The Adventist movement began with Bible prophecy; we are driven by it and know that Jesus is coming soon. Maranatha!

—*Vyacheslav Demyan, President, Hope Channel International*

A Message From Hope Studios

How could a war veteran, a 17-year-old girl in poor health, a penniless sea captain, and a widowed father in the 1800s reshape the world we live in today? Through the power of hope.

The story of these hopeful people has been inspiring tens of millions across the world, now brought to the big screen and in the book you're holding. It's a story of love and loss, war and rebellion, miracles and disappointments, and ultimately a search for truth.

The choices made by this unlikely cast of characters more than 150 years ago have led to an organized movement today that continues to impact our present world. It's a group rushing to the front lines of global disasters, saving lives in the largest Protestant-run health-care system in the world, educating future generations in schools/universities across continents, and even providing many of the healthy food products on our dinner tables. So when we were trying to decide what story to tell in feature film format on this scale, the choice for us at Hope Studios was obvious: we must tell the story of this now-22-million-member movement. Very few stories transcend nationalities, languages, cultures, and even historical periods on this scale.

Executive Producer of *The Hopeful*, Kevin Christenson, interviewed on It Is Written

The hardest part for us was choosing what stories to leave out of a 90-minute feature film; so we are glad to expand this saga, telling some of the untold stories through this book. May you experience the excitement, be stirred by the frustration, grieve with the heartbreak, and be inspired by the hope carried through today to become one of the hopeful.

—Kevin Christenson, Head of Hope Studios

A Word to the Reader

In the context of faith origin stories, few tales rival the compelling narrative of the early members of the Seventh-day Adventist movement. From great anticipation to great disappointment and through great perseverance, they paved the way for a 22-million-member movement that has changed the world.

The book you are about to read serves as a historical narrative companion to *The Hopeful* film, offering you an expanded journey into the lives of those who dared to stay hopeful. Their focus on Christ's character as a source of hope and healing continues today with the Adventist Development and Relief Agency (ADRA), one of the largest humanitarian and aid organizations globally, operating in more than 125 countries. Additionally, the movement operates the largest Protestant health-care network on the planet, with 500+ hospitals in 65 countries, along with schools, universities, literary publishers, and media organizations.

The Hopeful is more than a mere cinematic venture; it is a love letter to the people who, against all odds, embraced a vision of hope and perseverance. The Seventh-day Adventist movement emerged at a pivotal juncture in history, firmly anchoring faith with a commitment to health, education, and social justice. In this book we aim to illuminate the untold stories and sacrifices that laid the foundation for a community dedicated to revealing the true character of Christ to those around them.

To tell their story on film, I had the privilege of delving deep into the

archives, and in the personal correspondence between these early members, I discovered real and relatable people whose struggles and questions mirrored my own. This rich and vibrant community of real-life characters shaped the worldview I wrestled with as I left my teen years—a worldview I questioned the relevance of in my early 20s and, ultimately, a worldview I found a new understanding of and appreciation for in my 40s. In the lives of the early members, I didn't find people stagnant and afraid, elevating policy and rules above people. Instead I found people who were not afraid to move with the times—a people guided by present truth and willing to try new ways of bringing hope and healing to the community around them.

Through meticulous research and collaboration with historians, theologians, and descendants of the early members, we have endeavored to capture the essence of those transformative moments. Their story is a testament to the indomitable spirit of perseverance and the power of a shared vision.

I invite you to embark on this journey through time, to walk alongside those who dared to be different, to believe in the extraordinary, and to find hope in the face of uncertainty. May *The Hopeful* film and this accompanying narrative ignite a spark within you, reminding us all that even in the darkest hours there is a flicker of light—the light of hope that guides us through the corridors of history and into a future filled with promise.

—*Kyle Portbury, Emmy award-winning director of* The Hopeful

Contents

	A Word to the Reader	8
1	William and Lucy Miller *By Norma Collins*	11
2	Joshua Himes *By Melinda Worden*	27
3	Joseph and Prudence Bates *By Norma Collins*	37
4	Rachel Harris Oakes Preston *By Melinda Worden*	55
5	James White *By Norma Collins*	61
6	Ellen Gould Harmon *By Norma Collins*	75
7	James and Ellen White *By Norma Collins*	93
8	John Nevins Andrews *By Norma Collins*	121
9	Charles Melville Andrews *By Melinda Worden*	139
10	Mary Frances Andrews *By Melinda Worden*	147
	Bibliography	153

William Miller

"Today, Today, and Today, Till He Comes"

Red-faced and panting from his wild ride on his father's fastest horse, the young man rapped smartly on the back door of the Miller home. William Miller flung open the door to his nephew Irving Guliford, his sister's son.

"Why, Irv," exclaimed Miller in alarm, "whatever are you doing here, and so early in the morning? Is something wrong? How are your parents?"

Why would Irving be here so early?

"Oh, no, Uncle William," the boy eagerly replied, "everything's just fine. But Father sent me with a message, and oh, Uncle William, he let me ride his new horse. Is he ever fast! Man, we flew like the wind."

"Irv?" Miller said sternly, still a little apprehensive. "What's the message?"

"Oh, sorry," Irving apologized. "There's no preaching in our church tomorrow, and Father wants to know if you'll come and talk to our neighbors about the prophecies you've been studying. Will you come?"

Nothing could have shocked Miller more. Without a word he stormed out of the house and hurried up the little hill into the grove of maple trees that had become his refuge. He would not do it. *He could not.* But after a fierce battle with God, the farmer who went into the maple grove came out a preacher. Humbly he went home with his nephew. The following day, at Dresden, 16 miles from his home, he preached his first sermon on the second advent of Christ.

❖ ❖ ❖

The oldest of 16 children, William worked hard helping his father run the farm, but his great love was reading and learning. The family owned only three books: a Bible, a Psalter, and a Prayer Book—books that young William read over and over. But the time came when he wanted more, so he went about borrowing books from anyone in the neighborhood who had them. He had an insatiable curiosity to learn.

William Miller, just as Abraham Lincoln did many years later, stayed up after the family had gone to bed, then read into the wee hours of the morning. Candles were too expensive to waste for such frivolity as reading long into the night, but there were plenty of pine knots, and all he had to do was gather them from the woods. So it was that William formed the habit of burning "pine 'ots," as they were called locally, in the fireplace for his nightly reading light.

His highest priority was being sure there were plenty of pine 'ots on hand for his excursions into the world of learning. Always on the lookout for pine stumps that would make good light, he brought them to the wood lot and chopped them into the size and shape that best suited his nightly lighting requirements. He even commandeered a special hideaway where he stored the chunks of pine.

When William was a little older, his pine 'ots caused a commotion late one night. His father, also named William, felt that his son's late-night reading would cut into his energy and efficiency for the next day's work. And the farm required every ounce of work he could get from his son. He insisted that William retire for the night when the rest of the family did. And for all that his father knew, the growing boy slept soundly through the night, the same as everyone else.

William's "secret life" continued for some time. Night after night he read as long as he dared, then made his way back upstairs—avoiding the step that squeaked—and slept until it was time to do the morning chores. But one night he got something he hadn't bargained for. His father awoke and saw a glow downstairs. Thinking the house was on fire, he came rushing down the stairs to save his home and family from going up in flames. But instead of a house fire he saw his son William lying peacefully before the fireplace, reading some book he'd borrowed from a neighbor. His father grabbed his horse whip and took his son for a little chase around the room, using words that William remembered well for quite some time: "Young man, if you don't get to bed right now, I'm gonna horsewhip you!"

William went up to bed, at least for this night. He was only trying to get an education—a broader education than he could get from the teachers who came to their community during the first three or four months of winter, taught a few classes, and moved on.

It was this self-education that earned young Miller the distinction of being the community's "scribbler general."

And what is a scribbler general? Most of the people in that area were not very well educated, and a young man who wanted to say something special to a young lady usually didn't have the right words at his command to impress her. So these young suitors would come to Miller and describe the young lady they wanted to know better, and William would write flowery words and phrases that would make her heart go pitter-patter. The suitor would pass the note or poem along to the damsel of his choice as his own creation, and sometimes the fair heart was won.

LUCY, HIS LOVE

Growing up in isolated Low Hampton was a lonely experience. Eventually William found a summer job in Poultney, Vermont, a few miles from Low Hampton. There he met Miss Lucy Smith, and from that time on he often found excuses to visit Poultney. Miss Smith returned the romantic interest and became his bride.

They soon moved to her hometown, and wonder of wonders, Poultney had a library. It was the first village in Vermont to have a free public library, and William often could be found here, reading to his heart's content. Lucy knew she'd married a farm boy, and she thought that the more he read, the more refined he would become, and the better husband and father he would be. She encouraged her sweetheart to go to the library as often as possible. Unfortunately, it seems to be this library that introduced William to the writings of Voltaire, David Hume, Thomas Paine, and Ethan Allen—all considered great deist writers. He turned his back on religion and began to subscribe to the philosophy of deism. (Deists believe that God created a universe according to certain laws of cause and effect, put some people on this world, set it in motion, and then took no further interest in it.)

William began to meet with a group of deists in Poultney. His doubts about the Bible grew more and more serious, until he finally concluded that "the Bible was only the work of designing men, and I discarded it accordingly." He remained a deist for 12 years.

In spite of following deists views, William Miller was a man of high principles, fair-minded, and just. His neighbors and friends liked and trusted him. He became quite involved in politics, joining the Masons, and becoming an active Democrat. Year after year he was elected to local offices such as justice of the peace, constable, and deputy sheriff. An up-and-coming young man, he was on his way to being one of the most prominent citizens of Poultney.

In 1987 more than 1,000 documents—all in William Miller's own handwriting—were recovered from a barrel in the attic of his home in Low Hampton. Dating from the time Miller was a justice of the peace, the papers range from loans and repayment of loans, tax collection slips, and orders for arrest, to anything else that a justice of the peace might be called upon to adjudicate. They lay entombed in a barrel for 150 years or so, with no one being aware of the precious cache of history.[1]

WAR AND LOVE

Things were looking up for William and Lucy Miller, even though he'd given up his interest in religion. Then their world changed. The War of 1812 loomed large on the horizon, and while Miller had no interest in religion

he still had a strong sense of patriotism, duty, and honor. Naturally, when the president of the United States called for men to defend the honor of the United States, William—just as his father had done during the Revolutionary War—volunteered.

And now we see just how highly the Poultney community valued William. One of his duties was to collect taxes. He must have been a fair and reasonable collector, because when word came from the president that volunteers were needed to defend the United States, 47 men in Poultney said they would go on one condition. That condition was that William Miller—local tax collector, census taker, deputy sheriff, and all the other things he was—be appointed their officer. The original roster of those 47 men who signed their names to go to war with Captain William Miller now hangs in the William Miller home in Low Hampton, New York.

Before William left Lucy and home to go to war, the two of them agreed to write each other at least once a week. But Lucy wasn't quite the faithful letter writer that her husband thought she should be. Far from home, up near the Canadian border, he didn't hear from Lucy as often as he'd have liked. And so he wrote her this letter:

"Dear Lucy: Have you departed this life? Or are you so engaged that you could not devote one hour in a week to your humble servant? The following are the words you wrote me not long since. To wit, 'If I am alive I shall write to you weekly and put a letter in the post office every Monday morning.' Ever since Wednesday noon I have been dressed in mourning. Shall I ever see my Lucy again, I have often exclaimed. Ah, no! She could not tell me a falsehood. She must be dead. What can I write if she's gone? I cannot write anything; she cannot hear me. I can only write to my children, into whose hands I hope this letter will fall. Dear children, you have lost your mother and in but a little while your father must follow; perhaps before you receive this he will be no more. Prepare, then, my children, to meet the frowns of fortune, and learn, in your youth, to repel the shafts of adversity. . . .

"If Lucy is no more, or if she has forgotten Wm. Miller, then this letter is directed to Wm. S. Miller, his oldest son." Apparently, this note was sufficient to get the ink on Lucy's pen flowing again.

A captain in the United States Army, William was at the Battle of Plattsburg when a shell exploded within two feet of him and three other men. The others sustained injuries, but Miller walked away unscathed. At that notable moment, with the battle still raging, he didn't have time to wax philosophical. But that cannonball incident kept coming back to him, and he eventually realized that the God of heaven had protected him from harm.

THE GIFT OF RECONCILIATION

Not only had Miller been given the gift of a bright, inquiring mind, but he also seemed to have had the gift of reconciliation. He had a wonderful ability to persuade people to put aside their differences and work side by side.

Two men in his regiment had grown up in the same area, and had been the best of friends. During the war they'd remained friends and looked out for each other. Sometime later the two soldiers moved up near the Canadian border—probably near each other—and a major disagreement destroyed their friendship. Knowing how close they'd been and how unhappy they were to be enemies, possibly it was their families who suggested that they go see Captain Miller and ask him to be their mediator. After all, they both held him in high regard. Somewhere down deep in their souls they must have wanted to be friends again, for they agreed to this plan.

Having no other mode of transportation, the two former friends walked all the way to Miller's farm to ask him to help settle their differences. So sharp was their disagreement that rather than make the journey together they actually went by separate routes, each traveling alone, with only his hostile thoughts for company.

Of course, Captain Miller was glad to see them, but sorry they'd become such bitter enemies. As he listened to each of their stories, the God he didn't acknowledge gave him the wisdom to prevail on their common sense and fairness. After spending a few days at the Miller farm, and undoubtedly having several conversations with the good captain, the two traveled home together—once again good friends.

On another occasion, when one of the local political parties asked permission to hold its Fourth of July picnic on Miller's property, he persuaded the committee to invite the other political party to join in the fun too. And so the day of picnicking on Miller's farm became a holiday celebration rather than a political one.

He apparently had another gift—that of mimicking others in both voice and mannerisms. He used this "gift" to the considerable amusement of his friends and at the expense of several clergymen of his acquaintance, including his grandfather Phelps and his uncle Elihu. It's quite likely that his mischief wasn't limited to the clergy, and it does show that even though he was studious and serious, he had a wide streak of humor. It's not quite the picture we usually have of William Miller.

THE SERMON THAT CHANGED MILLER'S LIFE

After the death of Miller's father, William and Lucy moved back to Low Hampton so he could be near his mother and take care of her. While his years in the war had caused him to begin questioning the teachings of deism, he still didn't believe in a God who was personally interested in each of His created beings.

A devout Christian, his mother went to church every week. To please her, William sometimes attended church too. After all, a deist went to church so that he could be seen as honorable and upstanding in the community. And Miller wanted his wife and children in church. It was the proper thing to do. Besides, he didn't mind listening to Uncle Elihu speak on Sundays.

But when Uncle Elihu was called away to preach in one of his other churches, the deacons had to take turns reading the sermons from a book. The deacons weren't very well educated and didn't read very well, and Miller found it rather tedious to listen to them. When he knew his uncle was going to be absent from the pulpit, William didn't go to church with his mother.

One Sunday she asked him why he wasn't going, and he explained that it was a real chore for him to listen to the stumbling attempts of some of the men who were asked to read. He said that if *he* could read the sermons, then he certainly would be there.

Of course, Mrs. Miller did what any self-respecting mother would do under those circumstances. She let the board of deacons know that her son William would be willing to read the sermons on the days the preacher was absent. The deacons were delighted. It was a chore to them, too. From then on, when Uncle Elihu was in another of his churches, his deacons selected the Sunday sermon, and William Miller was pleased to read it.

Things continued in this way for quite some time—Miller still holding his deist views, and—although somewhat uncomfortably—reading the sermons on Sunday. He still considered Scripture just the writings of men.

On September 15, 1816, the deacons chose the reading titled "Importance of Parental Duties," a sermon written by Alexander Proudfit. But as Mr.

Miller read aloud, he suddenly broke down weeping, so overcome with emotion that he couldn't continue. He was forced to hand over the reading to one of those unlearned deacons and to take his seat in the congregation.

In this sermon Mr. Proudfit speaks of the way we should discipline children. He speaks about the fact that if we want our children to believe in God, we must believe. If we want them to believe in the value of prayer, we ourselves must believe in prayer. If we want them to get anything out of the worship service, we must go there expecting to get something out of it ourselves, and not just be there in body only.

It probably was on this point that the Holy Spirit was able to reach William Miller. God knew that he didn't believe in prayer, even though he sat through prayers at his home and in church. He knew he didn't believe there was any value in going to church, and yet he was there. He didn't believe in Bible study or anything that goes along with the Christian life. For a logical, rational-thinking deist, this would be a likely spot for the Holy Spirit to make contact with him. Miller could see the inconsistency of his own life.

Soon after this experience Miller wrote, "Suddenly the character of a Savior was vividly impressed upon my mind. It seemed that there might be a Being so good and compassionate as to Himself atone for our transgressions, and thereby save us from suffering the penalty of sin. I immediately felt how lovely such a Being must be; and imagined that I could cast myself into the arms of, and trust in the mercy of, such a One."

Later he said that "God opened my eyes; and Oh, my soul, what a Savior I discovered Jesus to be!"

He was forced to admit that the Bible presented just such a Savior as he needed, and that the "Scriptures must be a revelation from God."

He found that "the Scriptures became my delight, and in Jesus I found a friend." The Bible now became his chief study, and he searched it diligently. As he was going through all this change, Miller thought about the cannon shell that exploded so close to him, and yet he was not injured. He could come to no other conclusion than that there is a God who is interested in us as individuals; there is a God who does take an interest in the affairs of nations. And, yes, there is a God who looks after each person, and who loved him—William Miller.

Beginning with Genesis 1:1, he began to study his Bible in every spare moment. He didn't use any commentaries or Bible dictionaries, or any books that had been written about the Scriptures. He wanted only to find out what kind of God the Bible itself revealed.

For the next two years—1816 to 1818—using only his Bible and his *Cruden's Concordance*, Miller worked his way through the Scriptures. When he came across a word he didn't understand, he would look it up in his concordance, and then look up each of the texts that used that particular word. By the time he had looked at all the words in their context he knew how the Bible used that word.

It was during this time that Miller discovered the 2300-day prophecy of

Daniel 8:14: "Unto two thousand and three hundred days; then shall the sanctuary be cleansed." As he studied and pondered and allowed the Holy Spirit to lead him, he came to the conclusion that the earth was the sanctuary to be cleansed by fire when Jesus comes.

He had fallen in love with Jesus, fallen in love with the Bible! He put it like this: "I saw the Bible did bring to view just such a Savior as I needed, and I was perplexed to find out how an uninspired book should develop principles so perfectly adapted to the wants of a fallen world. I was constrained [forced!] to admit that the Scriptures must be a revelation from God. They became my delight, and in Jesus I found a friend."

His deep love for his new Friend, Jesus Christ, was the force that kept him going when he began to preach the soon coming of Jesus. As he studied the Scriptures he arrived at the conclusion that Jesus would come about 25 years from that time. Jesus, his newfound friend, was going to come back to earth in about 25 years! Being an honest man, Miller studied and restudied his findings. By 1818 he had concluded that Christ would come about 1843.

For the next 13 years the conviction grew that he must tell others of the soon coming of his Best Friend, Jesus, but he didn't want to leave his home to preach. He didn't want to be made fun of, to be the butt of jokes. Oh, he had lots of reasons for not going public. He finally did come to the point where he was willing to talk with people one on one, but remained unwilling to stand up and preach to an audience.

THE HOPEFUL **WILLIAM MILLER**

HE TALKED OF NOTHING ELSE

It was about this time that a physician in the neighborhood began to say that William Miller was a monomaniac. We've already established that he was well respected and well liked in the community, so probably the physician didn't really mean any harm. He just didn't like hearing even a little bit of Miller's findings about the Bible, so he was known to say something to this effect: "We all like Esquire Miller [a title of respect], but when you get him started on this prophecy business, he's nothing but a monomaniac."

In other words, when you get him going, he's way off base on this prophecy business. Of course, the danger of saying things behind someone's back is well known—some kindly soul will tell him what's being said. And that's what happened in this case. Someone squealed on the good doctor.

We've already seen a little glimpse of Miller's humor in that exchange of letters with his wife. So now let's see how he handled the situation with the doctor who said he was a monomanic on the prophecies.

With 10 children in the family, it wasn't too long before one of them became ill, and that same doctor was called to attend the child. He took care of the youngster and was about to make a quick escape. He certainly didn't want to get into a discussion with Esquire Miller.

But there he sat beside the door, looking rather ill—in fact, he was doing his best to look as ill as possible.

The doctor asked if there was something wrong with him, and Miller admitted that maybe there was, but he didn't know just what. The physician checked his pulse, and that seemed to be all right. So he asked Miller what he thought the problem might be.

"Well," Miller replied, "I'm not totally sure, but could it be that I'm a monomaniac?" The doctor had the grace to turn all shades of the rainbow.

But Miller kept on. "Doctor, would you know a monomaniac if you really saw one?"

"Yes, I think I would."

"Then I'd like you to examine me to find out if I'm really a monomaniac. If I am, I want to be treated for it—for my peace of mind, for my mental health."

There was no way out for the poor, embarrassed doctor. How could he give an examination for such an ailment? As he was looking for a way to get past Mr. Miller and out the door, he heard Miller say, "Oh, and Doctor, feel free to charge your regular fee for this examination."

Of course, Miller knew that the only way Doctor X could examine him for this particular ailment was for Miller himself to give the doctor a Bible study. He was so concerned about that man's soul that it was worth it to pay for an examination just so he could sit down with him and describe from Daniel why he thought the 2300-day prophecy was about to end, and Jesus was about to return.

Escape seemed impossible. At last the doctor sat down, and one by one Miller went through all those familiar texts in Daniel. Gradually, as they worked out the chronology, Doctor X saw that it wasn't just a bunch of mumbo-jumbo. It actually made sense. He was so agitated that he jumped up and ran out the door. William Miller smiled in anticipation of their next meeting—which came even sooner than he expected. Bright and early the next morning there was a knock at the door.

When William saw him, he exclaimed, "Why, Doctor, you look like you haven't slept a wink all night."

"No, I haven't," replied the doctor. "If all you've told me is true, I have to know more. I'm not ready to go to heaven. You need to study with me until I know all there is to know."

So Doctor X and Mr. Miller arranged to have more Bible studies. By the end of the studies the doctor went away rejoicing—as much a monomaniac on the prophecies as William Miller himself.

Yet Miller was not willing to go public with his findings. With the prodding of the Holy Spirit, the certainty was growing that he should—indeed, *must*—go and tell it to the world. But who, he reasoned, would listen to a farmer preach that Jesus was coming soon?

Sometimes the Lord, to get His children to do something they should, has to start convicting them far in advance of His timetable for getting it done. For 13 years the Holy Spirit had been urging him to share his findings that Jesus was coming soon. Still Miller struggled, back and forth, unwilling to commit himself to preaching the good news of his findings.

But the Holy Spirit wouldn't let him off the hook. As he went about his business, he continually heard the words ringing in his ears: "Go and tell the world of their danger."

Finally giving up in despair, he told the Lord that he would go and preach if anyone asked him. He felt perfectly safe in making this promise because he felt quite sure no one would ask a 50-year-old farmer to preach on the second coming of the Lord. But God's clock was ticking. The time had come, and God had a surprise for Farmer Miller.

You see, it was within a half hour of his promise to the Lord that his nephew Irving Guliford knocked at the door with the invitation for Miller to come to Dresden and preach.

And there in the maple grove, like Jacob of old, Miller wrestled and argued with the Lord. He'd promised he would go if invited; but he hadn't expected to be invited! Now he tried to find a way out of his promise to the Lord.

At last, reason prevailed. Even as a deist he had been a man of his word, and God surely knew that. Whatever he said he would do, he did.

He finally submitted, promising God that if the Lord would sustain him, he would go. It was God, not Miller himself, who wanted him to preach. The following day, at Dresden, he preached his first sermon on the Second Advent. The meetinghouse was well filled, and the audience attentive. At first Miller was uncomfortable and nervous, but as soon as he began speaking his unease vanished.

The interest was so great that the people of Dresden asked him to stay through the following week and give lectures every day. With every passing day more people came from neighboring towns to hear the good news that Jesus was coming soon. A revival began, and it was said that in 13 families all but two persons were converted.

Arriving home the following week, Miller found a letter from a pastor in Poultney, Vermont, asking him to lecture in his church on the same subject. That pastor hadn't heard of the Dresden experience, and from that time on, invitations poured in for the 50-year-old farmer to preach on the second coming of Jesus. The word was out that if a pastor wanted a great revival series, William Miller was the man who would draw big crowds with good results.

Miller's reputation as "the greatest evangelistic influence in the northeastern United States between 1840 and 1844" is well deserved. But no man is an island, and he didn't act alone.

TO THE CITIES

Joshua V. Himes entered the picture in 1839. He heard Miller preach and believed his message. Himes himself would continue to spread that message until his death at the age of 91. Miller had been going only to the towns and villages where he had been invited. *But what about the cities?* Himes wondered. He asked Miller if he would preach in cities if he had an invitation, and the answer was yes.

Himes seemed to be a public relations genius. He started the Millerite *Signs of the Times*, and he edited the *Millennial Harp*, a collection of Second Advent hymns. He ran a column in the paper that printed all the falsehoods about Miller's teachings, and urged people to send in their evidence of false teaching or claims. He was an organizer par excellence and gave the Millerite movement the structure and leadership it needed as it became a mighty force directed by God Himself.

Another of Miller's followers was Josiah Litch—a Methodist preacher whose life was transformed when he heard the message of Christ's soon return. Litch became the leading Millerite theologian, writing pamphlets and books, and editing at least one Advent newspaper, *Trumpet of Alarm*.

And there were others. Millerism was a team effort. Its leaders represented different states, different churches, and different personality types. Each person made a significant contribution to the movement. They did their best to prepare a people for Christ's soon return.

At the beginning of this chapter is a picture of William Miller, but a few words may add understanding to the following story. When he was about

62, Miller's personal appearance was described as being about medium height and a little overweight. He had blue eyes that regarded one with an expression of kindhearted warmth. Even at 62, his hair was not gray, but a light auburn; his voice was full and distinct. But his head shook as though he had palsy. His dress was plain and ordinary.

A certain pastor, Timothy Cole, in Lowell, Massachusetts, hearing of Miller's work and of its results, invited him to come and preach in his church. He'd never met Miller, but expected to see a fashionably dressed gentleman when he went to the depot to meet him. He had heard that Miller wore a camel cloak and a white hat.

At the train station Timothy Cole stood on the platform closely inspecting everybody who got off the train. Not one man fit his image of Mr. Miller. Finally, he watched the last person step down from the train— an old man, shaking with palsy.

No, no, he thought. *No. This can't be the William Miller.*

But . . . this man *did* have a white hat and a camel cloak. Fearing that this indeed might be Mr. Miller, and if so, regretting that he had invited him to lecture in *his* church, Cole stepped up to him and whispered in his ear, "Is your name Miller?"

Miller nodded.

With a sigh, Cole said, "Well, follow me."

And he walked on ahead, leaving Mr. Miller to keep up the best he could until they finally reached the Cole home. There was no conversation. Cole neither asked him whether he'd had a good trip nor thanked him for coming. There were no pleasantries at all. Cole was embarrassed that he had invited a man of Miller's appearance. Surely this man could know nothing of the Bible; his lecture would be his own fancies.

They probably had some kind of light supper—perhaps soup and a sandwich, with a cup of something warm to drink. Kind, loving William Miller, shaking with palsy, was doing his best to eat his soup without spilling it. The conversation was sparse, limited to the most basic necessities. It was a great trial to all concerned. Cole was mentally kicking himself for having to deal with what he felt certain was a mistake, while Miller sat at the table of his ungracious host knowing he was unwelcome and trying to control his trembling hands and not spill his food and drink. Perhaps Cole's wife tried to put Miller at ease. It can only be hoped that she had a little more compassion than her husband did at that point.

After they ate, Pastor Cole told Mr. Miller that he supposed it was about time to go to the church. Again, he strode ahead without regard for his visitor. At the church Cole showed his guest to the platform, but took his seat with the congregation. He did not even introduce the visiting speaker. Miller was on his own in a strange congregation, with no support from the minister who'd invited him. It was an awkward situation to say the least.

In his strong, mellow voice, Mr. Miller read a hymn. After it was sung, he prayed and read another hymn, which also was sung. To say that he felt uncomfortable at being left on the platform alone would be a gross understatement. But he plowed ahead and read his text. It was his favorite: "Looking for that blessed hope, and the glorious appearing of the great God and our Savior Jesus Christ."

Launching into his sermon, Miller forgot all the unpleasantness as he warmed to his topic. He spoke with authority, proving all his points from the Scriptures. Timothy Cole listened for about 15 minutes, then seeing that only the Word of God was presented—with authority—and that the Scriptures were opened in a knowledgeable way, he walked up and took his seat on the platform.

Was Timothy Cole thoroughly ashamed of himself for the callous way he had treated God's servant? Did he make humble apologies for his lack of hospitality in the pulpit, as well as in his home? If he did, William Miller accepted them, for he was a true Christian gentleman.

The matter surely must have been smoothed over, because Miller spoke in Cole's church for nine days that May, and during another six days in June. A wonderful revival followed, and in late July Cole wrote to Mr. Miller that about 60 people had joined the church.

Timothy Cole learned that one cannot always judge the measure of a man by his outward appearance.

In early 1844 Miller himself reported that during the past 12 years he had preached about 4,500 sermons to at least 500,000 people. It was his chief aim to tell others of his Best Friend, Jesus. Nothing was more precious to him than the thought of Christ's soon return. Although Miller's mistaken belief that Jesus would return about 1843 or 1844 gave an urgency to his preaching, time was not his entire message. He longed for people to accept Jesus as their personal Savior and to be ready to meet Him when He returned—whenever that would be. From the time of his conversion—that Sunday when he read that sermon at his mother's church—his life revolved around being with Jesus and doing all in his power to help others be ready for His return.

Miller and his fellow preachers labored on and on, warning the world of the soon coming of Christ. But October 22, 1844, came and went without the appearance of the Lord Jesus. There was mighty disappointment throughout the ranks.

Actually, William Miller accepted the October 22 date only about two weeks before the time. In all his preaching he had been reluctant to give an exact date for the Second Advent. He preached a constant readiness, whatever the day. And that was the tenor of a letter to his old friend Joshua V. Himes, about two weeks after the Disappointment:

"I have fixed my mind upon another time, and here I mean to stand until God gives me more light—And that is *Today, Today,* and *Today,* until He comes."

In 1848 Miller had a small chapel[2] built on his farm, close to his house, where those who continued to be loyal to the Advent message could worship. Most of them had been disfellowshipped from the churches in which they had had membership, as he himself had been.

About that same time Miller began to lose his sight. One of his greatest sorrows came the day he could no longer see to read and write. As a boy he'd read by the light of pine 'ots in the fireplace. When he married and moved to Poultney, he'd reveled in the many books its public library held. At last he could read all he wanted to. And now the privilege of reading his beloved Bible was denied him. His daughter-in-law knew how hard this was for him, but reported that he never complained. His Best Friend was Jesus, and Jesus helped him to bear this cross with grace.

He wrote to his close friend Joshua V. Himes:

"It would, indeed, be a sad and melancholy time with me were it not for the 'blessed hope' of soon seeing Jesus. Although my natural vision is dark, yet my mind's vision is lit up with a bright and glorious prospect for the future." After the disappointment of 1844, William Miller was never really well. From then on his health steadily declined. Sometimes he became better, even going out to preach, but finally his last illness came upon him. When it seemed that Miller was near death, a telegram was sent to Joshua Himes. He arrived on December 17, and although Mr. Miller was very ill, he recognized Himes's voice. He could hardly believe his old friend was there, and kept exclaiming, "Oh, is it really you, Elder Himes? Is it really Elder Himes? Oh, I'm so glad to see you." He spoke of the Advent cause, of their work together, and charged his friend to be faithful in his duties.

On his last day, Miller was not able to talk much. But from time to time uttered expressions such as "Mighty to save!" "Oh, I long to be there," and "Victory! Victory!" The glorious scenes going through his mind can only be imagined. Surely the Lord was very near to him during those final hours of his life. He fell asleep in Jesus on December 20, 1849, without seeing his fondest hope realized.

He was laid to rest in the Low Hampton cemetery, just a little distance from his home. There he awaits the call of his Best Friend. On his tombstone is a quotation from Daniel 12:13: "But go thou thy way till the end be: for thou shalt rest, and stand in thy lot at the end of the days."

Ellen White, shown God's eventual reward for His dedicated servant, wrote: "Angels watch the precious dust of this servant of God, and he will come forth at the sound of the last trump."

On the great resurrection day, Miller will realize his heart's desire: to be with his Friend, Jesus, to "see his Lord a-coming."

---

[1] Samples can be seen at the Ellen G. White Estate.

[2] That small chapel remains today. It's owned by the Advent Christian Church, and is jointly maintained by them and the Seventh-day Adventist Church. Tour groups and others visit there on a regular basis, especially during the summer months.

Vignette

MR. PHRENOLOGIST

A phrenologist supposedly was able to "read" the bumps on a person's head, and thereby learn of the person's character and capabilities. It was something that was popular during the early 1800s and seemingly harmless. Often there was an audience as these examinations were being made.

William Miller was a man with a mission—a mission to tell others that Jesus was coming soon. Along the way he met many interesting people and had many varied experiences. On one occasion, in 1842, a new convert talked Miller into visiting a phrenologist.

As the phrenologist examined his unknown client's head, he began to joke about what he thought William Miller's head might be like. Knowing that the man who had brought in the anonymous client was a Millerite, the phrenologist declared, "Mr. Miller couldn't easily convert *this* man to his harebrained theory. He has too much good sense."

The examiner suggested that this fine head was just the opposite of what Miller's head was. His audience smiled as he exclaimed, "Oh, how I should like to examine Mr. Miller's head. I would give it one good squeezing!"

Knowing who the client was, those watching the procedure had a good laugh. The phrenologist joined merrily in the laughter, thinking they appreciated his jokes. When he finished the examination and made out his chart, he said to his client, "And what is your name, sir?"

The poor man had already made a fool of himself, and Miller didn't want to embarrass him further, so he modestly said, "Oh, the name doesn't matter."

But Mr. Phrenologist insisted. He had to have a name on the chart. "Very well," came the reluctant reply. "You may call it Miller." "Miller, Miller," Mr. Phrenologist murmured as he filled in the chart.

"And what is your first name?"

"Well, they call me William Miller," Miller quietly replied.

"What! The gentleman who is lecturing in Boston?"

"Yes sir, the same."

At this the phrenologist turned pale, fell back in his chair, and didn't have another word to say.

Joshua Himes

Promoter With Passion

"So do you *really* believe this?" Joshua Himes kept his eyes locked on William Miller's as he bluntly discharged the question.

"Yes, I do," came Miller's firm and clear reply.

It was December 1839, and William Miller was holding a series of meetings, preaching the Advent message to Joshua Himes's congregation at the Chardon Street Chapel in Boston, Massachusetts. The invitation to speak first came as a written request, and then Himes renewed the request in person to Miller the month before at a Christian ministers' conference in Exeter, New Hampshire.

"But why have you not been to the large cities?" His voice was incredulous, his eyes wide and full of eagerness.

"My rule has been to visit only those places where I am invited, and I have not received an invitation to any of the large cities." William's calm tone didn't dampen Joshua's excitement.

"Well, will you go with me where the doors are opened?"

"Yes, I am ready to go anywhere and labor to the extent of my ability to the end." Again, the words were said clearly, yet with a humbled calmness.

"Prepare for the campaign! For doors should be opened in every city in the union, and the warning should go to the ends of the earth!" Miller wasn't so sure about this. It was one thing to be invited by small groups scattered around in the small towns and villages. Why would large groups gather in the cities just to hear this message?

Himes's enthusiasm rang true, and it wasn't long before any doubts that William Miller had about his ability to open doors had vanished.

When Joshua Himes put his mind to something, he made it happen. He was a born influencer and publicist. His energy and charisma drew people to him. His God-given talent to promote and market was just the resource needed to spread the word quickly!

❖ ❖ ❖

Joshua Vaughan Himes was born May 19, 1805, in North Kingston, Rhode Island. His father, Stukely Himes, a West India trader and a prominent member of the Episcopal Church, had done financially well for his family. He had planned that his son would attend Brown University in Providence, Rhode Island, to be educated for the Episcopal ministry. But those plans quickly evaporated when in 1817 the ship captain that Mr. Himes had hired turned against him. The crooked captain sold the ship and all its goods, then disappeared. This disaster devastated the Himes family financially and changed the course of young Joshua's life forever. Attending Brown University was now out of reach. Instead, his father apprenticed him to a New Bedford cabinetmaker.

The eight years in New Bedford allowed Joshua to attend the meetings of the Christian Church. By age 18 he had become a member. His fellow members saw and encouraged his talent for speaking, and within a short time he was conducting evangelistic services.

Joshua wasn't one to move at a slow pace. His 20s began with an end to his apprenticeship and the beginning of his life as a full-fledged pastor. At 21 he married Mary Thompson Hardy, and just one year later he raised a church in Fall River, Massachusetts, with 125 members!

Before he reached the age of 30, he had gone to Boston as the pastor of the Christian church there. The membership had shrunk to an embarrassingly low attendance. Within two years his energy and love for the Lord filled the church to the point of full capacity!

Joshua brought people to the Lord, but he also strongly encouraged reform. He wholeheartedly "fought a good fight" (2 Timothy 4:7, KJV). He spoke out against the use of liquor and against slavery. The reforms brought him into the company of other like-minded reformers, such as Joseph Bates and William Lloyd Garrison. Garrison went on to form the William Lloyd Garrison's New England Anti-Slavery Society. He praised Joshua for being steadfast and true to the full and immediate ceasing of slavery, right from the start, and not backing down when faced with opposition. His members of the Chardon Street Chapel in Boston knew that their pastor was straightforward, energetic, and passionate about his beliefs!

A NEW CAUSE

Joshua Himes's passion for reform and the betterment of life met its peak when he fully embraced the Second Advent message. That the Lord would come and make a new earth was exactly what this sin-sick world needed.

He was 34 and in the prime of his life. He was known for his stylish clothes, charming personality, and an air of confidence and assurance. By

THE HOPEFUL **JOSHUA HIMES**

all accounts he was honest and sincere. He was noted to be a restless and energetic crusader!

When William Miller accepted Himes's invitation to speak at the Chardon Street Chapel in December 1839, Himes was happy to have Miller stay at his house during the series. This afforded Himes ample time to be able to have one-on-one conversations with Miller and pore over their Bible studies. The two did not always see eye to eye on every point, but they respected each other's opinion and agreed to disagree.

THE POWER OF PUBLISHING

One idea that William Miller had had since he began his ministry was to be able to have a source of communication other than just speaking and seminars. He knew they needed a written form where people could read what he had to say, instead of reading his critics. Joshua immediately agreed, and on March 20, 1840, Himes started the *Signs of the Times* paper. He was the editor and in charge of marketing and obtaining subscriptions, all without a salary. To get the project started, he contracted with an antislavery printer who agreed to cover the production costs and retain the profit for the first year. Himes was able to gain 1,500 subscribers in the first year! He renegotiated his agreement with the printer: they would be hired as the printer, but the profit would be put toward furthering the Second Advent message. By the next year the subscriptions had jumped to 5,000! The hope was that the paper would continue to promote prayer, Bible study, revivals, and awareness of the Lord's second coming.

Next Himes took on the role of publisher. He gathered Miller's lectures; he had charts, stationery, pamphlets, songbooks, tracts, books, and more! He took great financial risks with these printing ventures, for some were working just as hard against the cause.

Himes used the tools that were available to him. He placed stacks of printed materials in heavily populated places, such as the post office and newspaper office, and to share the message even further, he sent bundles with sailors who could leave them at their destination points.

One city that Joshua Himes wanted to reach was New York. In 1842 a big evangelistic campaign was launched there. It was clear to Himes that speaking and publishing went hand in hand. Himes went to work on a paper for the event, the *Midnight Cry*. Ten thousand copies were printed daily and sold or (more often) given away by newsboys during the evangelistic series. The paper's success was so great that it continued as a weekly. The continuation of the paper also happened in other large cities. The distribution during the campaign was not a moneymaking venture at all, but it was money well spent.

CAMP MEETINGS

"We need a larger space for the meetings. Too many times our locations are overflowing," one Advent pastor said, addressing his fellow Advent believers during their first general conference, held in the Chardon Street Chapel.

The assembly had agreed that they would not be officially organized, and each respected the various and different doctrinal beliefs. They were united by their common belief in the Lord's second coming. It was May 1842, and the feeling of urgency could be felt by all!

"I agree! The time is fast approaching! We need to do something big." The pressing plea could be heard in the preacher's voice.

"Yes! We need to have one of those tent meetings," responded another.

The assembly confirmed the decision, and plans were quickly made. Joshua Himes was once again at the forefront of the endeavor. He was a man of action, and once he had a direction, he didn't waste time in accomplishing his task. By the last week in June 1842, the first camp meeting of Adventists was held.

True to form, Himes had everything efficiently arranged. The location, East Kingston, Massachusetts, was close to the Boston and Portland Railroad, with access to water and large hemlock trees for shade, and could offer a quiet place for personal prayer and devotions. People from all over New England attended, anywhere from 7,000 to 10,000, and all kept peace and harmony.

"Yes. I need it to be 120 feet in diameter." Joshua repeated the order to the tentmaker. "We need to be able to have thousands sit under it."

"That means the center pole will be 55 feet high . . ." The man had been scribbling the order and then working the numbers to finish the dimensions. "Are you sure? That's the biggest tent we've ever made."

"PERFECT!" Joshua flashed him a bright smile.

The tent quickly became famous and was called "the great tent." The group took it all over the area. Often people came to see it and then would stay for the meetings. It was said of Himes: "He spread more canvas than any circus in America."

For the next two years the group of Advent believers were able to put together 125 camp meetings, reaching anywhere from 500,000 to 1 million attendees. The great tent was not able to be at each event, but it made its way to as many as possible!

A DATE IS SET

"He said what?" Joshua Himes stared at William Miller with disbelief. "You leave them alone for a few months, and this happens." Sighing and shaking his head, he turned from Miller.

Miller and Himes had just returned from a hugely successful evangelistic series done in the West, otherwise known as Cincinnati, Ohio. Himes had arranged for the great tent to be there, as well as to have the area blanketed with the *Western Midnight Cry* and other publications. Other camp meetings were taking place in the New England area, one being in Exeter, New Hampshire. At this meeting a fellow Advent believer, S. S. Snow, presented his idea that Christ would return at the regular time for the Jewish cleansing of the sanctuary, which corresponded to October 22, 1844.

At first both Miller and Himes were opposed to fixing a date. Any paper owned by Himes did not support this idea. The idea of an exact date rushed in like a tidal wave, covering the area with great speed and intensity, catching everyone up in it! Again, Himes was not immediately convinced, but he could not ignore the rapid movement and results. It brought him to reexamine his studies.

"We are now less than a month away from the predicted day. I cannot ignore or deny the intense power that adding a date has done to this message. This must be a supernatural force. With so many turning to their Bibles, it must be of the Lord, and we should not stand against it." Joshua Himes searched William Miller's face for a clue as to how he was feeling.

"I follow your line of thinking. I pray that it is correct," came William's calm, quiet reply.

Joshua Himes didn't shy away from confrontation, and he didn't shy away from admitting his own imperfection, the pride in his own opinions and self, and his slowness to receive new truths. In early October he did just that and continued his tireless effort to tell as many people as he could about the Lord's soon return.

For the next few weeks it was as if someone had turned over an hourglass and the sand was falling fast. People did whatever they felt they needed to do to make themselves right with the Lord and others. Shop owners and farmers didn't worry about inventory or fields; some sold or gave away everything they had, and all were counting the days and keeping their eyes on the sky. Joshua Himes was there in the middle of the chaos, keeping the presses turning out as many final warning messages as they had ink and paper for. By October 19 he had made his way from Boston to Low Hampton, New York. He wanted to share the joyous Advent with his close friend, William Miller.

October 22 arrived as a bright, beautiful day in New York. When it ended, there was a cloud of sadness hanging thick in the air. The Lord had not come.

It certainly wasn't easy to be an Advent believer then. The extreme depression that they must have felt! First, not to be with the Lord in heaven; and second, to have to face all the scoffers and ridiculers. Often these distraught members were met with verbal and physical abuse. Some of the meetinghouses were burned or vandalized.

"I told you that Himes was up to no good! Running around with that big tent! Scaring people into giving him all their money. For what? Look at them now. What a shame."

"Doesn't he feel the least bit guilty? Lying to people, taking their money, and now leaving them sad and penniless. Disgusting."

The negative comments and accusations were everywhere, spoken loudly, whispered, written, or in cartoons. Joshua Himes was right in the middle of it, specifically being accused of making up the Advent and keeping back funds for personal financial gain.

But amid all this, Joshua Himes didn't back down or hide away! He stood firm as an Advent leader and did what he could to rally the spirits of his disheartened and oppressed members. Staying emotionally strong and not losing his belief in the return of the Lord, he immediately went back to work, starting the *Advent Herald*, the successor to the *Signs of the Times*. He also resumed the *Midnight Cry*, changing its title to *Morning Watch*.

His first message was to encourage the Advent believers with material possessions to take care of their fellow Advent believers who were left without anything. He was specifically worried about the fast-approaching winter, wanting them to stay fed and warm, and not dependent on those who were mocking and ridiculing them.

Those first few months were very difficult ones. William Miller and Joshua Himes reaffirmed their belief in the Advent, but emphasized that it was not something that should have a specific date. By the spring the two had once again put together a convention of Advent leaders, in Albany, New York. Miller was the chair and Himes the secretary.

Himes worked hard to keep some of the new and confusing religious beliefs out of Adventism. He wanted the focus to remain on the Second

Coming. It was too much to be taking tangents down paths of religious practices that seemed to simply distract from being prepared for Christ's return. He gathered the leaders together and discussed the core principles of Adventism and how to best share this still-important message. It was time to build again!

MOVING FORWARD

Joshua Himes continued his work in publishing. He continued to publish the *Advent Herald* for some years. He moved to the West and published the *Voice of the West* at Buchanan, Michigan, and later the *Advent Christian Times* in Chicago.

A small group of Adventists had begun to study the Bible further, specifically the fourth commandment. They joined the seventh-day Sabbath with the Advent message. Joshua wasn't sure of this and decided to keep his beliefs solely rooted in the Advent. At times he was at odds with this new group, but both could agree to disagree on some points and heartily agree on others.

Until his death on July 27, 1895, Himes gave of himself to supporting and helping those around him. He continued publishing, pastoring, and fighting for human rights. He very much wanted to influence the world to be a better place.

In his later years in life Himes became ill with cancer and went to the Battle Creek Sanitarium, where he remained for a long course of treatment. Himes found this treatment to help, not only physically, but mentally and spiritually. There he was able to enjoy socializing and receiving visits with old friends from the Advent movement. They remembered and respected his impressive leadership!

During this time, when Himes was 90 years old, the Seventh-day Adventists in Battle Creek invited him to join them at the camp meeting that they were holding there. He spoke in the large tent to a massive crowd.

"We must prepare! The Lord will soon return, and we must be ready!" His voice carried the same fire and passion that he had had from the first days of preaching the Advent message!

His bones creaked a little as he made his way back to his seat. Slowly lowering himself onto his chair, Himes let out a slow breath. Closing his eyes, he could smell the canvas of the tent and hear the excitement of the crowd. *If only Father Miller were here!* He could almost feel him sitting beside him, getting ready to next take the podium. Opening his eyes, he thanked the Lord for the kindness and acceptance this group, with whom he didn't always agree, showed him. It was truly a great gift to have the chance to share Christ's return one more time!

Joshua Himes's obituary was written by Seventh-day Adventist and *Review and Herald* editor Uriah Smith, who said: "All through that movement [the 1844 movement] he was the leading and most aggressive human instrumentality, pushing on the cause of publishing, preaching, and organizing the various enterprises connected with that work. Mr. Miller acknowledged and appreciated his great services, and Seventh-day Adventists have always respected and honored him for the noble part he acted in that great prophetic religious awakening."

THE HOPEFUL **JOSHUA HIMES**

PAINTED BY J. B. FLAGG   ENGRAVED BY J. SARTAIN

JOSHUA HIMES

Joseph Bates

Herald of the Sabbath

The long, sleek shark followed the cargo ship *Fanny* all day, always keeping to the same side of the ship. The shark was savvy enough to keep out of spearing range, and although the sailors tried everything they knew to get rid of it, they were unsuccessful. One of the many superstitions regarding the sea was that when a shark follows a ship someone will either die or fall overboard. Not a few of the men on the *Fanny* believed these superstitions.

Late in the afternoon, the officer in charge sent young Joseph (not yet very experienced) up one of the masts to scan the sea for other vessels. Seeing nothing, he began his descent. Somehow he slipped, lost his footing, and fell toward the deck. At the last instant he hit a rope, and instead of crashing to almost certain death on the deck, he was thrown into the sea. Down, down, down into the depths he plunged.

"Man overboard! Man overboard!" shouted one of the deckhands who had seen him fall.

Rushing to the stern, the captain and his men searched the swirling waters in the wake of the ship. There was no sign of the seaman who had fallen. The weight of his clothing, especially his boots, dragged Joseph far down into the water. After what seemed to him an eternity, he popped back to the surface, but his clothes were so waterlogged that he couldn't swim. The ship continued to press ahead, and his chances of rescue were dwindling fast.

Fortunately, one of the officers spotted him among the foaming waves, and with all the strength he could muster threw a coiled rope toward the drowning boy. Exhausted as he was, Joseph knew this was his only chance.

He caught the rope with his last remnant of strength and hung on for dear life—literally—as the men pulled him through the roiling water and hauled him up to the deck. He could only lie there, gasping for breath.

In his terror of drowning, Joseph hadn't thought about the shark, but the deadly creature had been uppermost in the minds of some of the men, for Joseph had fallen right where the shark had been all day. The seamen looked over the side. The dark form was no longer there. Rushing to the other side of the ship, they saw the shark's glistening body still keeping pace with the ship. It apparently was unaware of the juicy meal it had missed by changing its course.

While the sailors were tracking the shark, Joseph was taken to the small cabin that served as a sick bay. There he was briskly rubbed dry with rough towels and wrapped in blankets. As he lay in the hammock, recovering from his close call with death, he thought about his mother. Though he hadn't bothered to read it, he knew she'd tucked a small Bible into his bag when he'd left home. The thought flashed into his mind that it was quite probable that she was praying for him at the time of his fall from the mast and the plunge into the cold, churning waters. He couldn't help wondering if God had sent the shark to the other side of the ship.

DESTINED FOR THE SEA

The fifth of seven children, Joseph Bates spent his early years amid the sights, sounds, and smells of New Bedford, Massachusetts—at that time the major whaling center of the world. He and his friends spent every minute they could at the docks. They were familiar with all the ships and on friendly terms with the men who sailed them. Joseph could hardly wait until he was old enough to join them as they sailed to exotic lands. His love affair with the sea, ships, and mystic lands was already well established. It was said that the population of New Bedford was divided into three parts—those who were away on a voyage, those who had just returned, and those who were getting ready to embark.

Joseph was almost 15, and his mother and father weren't having much success as they tried to persuade him to follow some other career. Mr. Bates had been a soldier, serving with General Washington at Valley Forge. He thought perhaps a career in the Army would be better than one at sea. But Joseph had only one desire—to sail the boundless seas and see the wonderful sights of foreign ports.

In desperation, Mr. Bates suggested to his wife that they let Joseph go on a short trip up the coast, perhaps to Boston. Maybe that would get it out of his system. Maybe he would get so seasick that he would never again want to board a ship. Maybe. His uncle owned a small cargo ship, and arrangements were made for Joseph to sail with him on his next trip to Boston.

But the short voyage only whetted his appetite for more. Joseph's big grin told his parents that the trip had been everything he'd hoped for, and that this was the life for him. Bowing to the inevitable, Mr. and Mrs. Bates looked for a ship—more accurately, a ship's captain—to whom they could entrust their young son.

Unfortunately for them, at that very moment a new ship, the *Fanny*, was being readied to sail. It was bound for London by way of New York, where it would take on a load of wheat. The captain was an able and kind man, who gave his word to Joseph's parents that he personally would be responsible for his new cabin boy.

The next few days were a whirlwind of activity as both ship and boy made final preparations for the beginning of their respective careers. Much too soon Mr. and Mrs. Bates stood on the dock watching the *Fanny* disappear into the distance. With heavy hearts they turned toward home. There was no guarantee that they'd see their son again. In that long-ago time there was no quick way to communicate. It could be months—even years—before they'd hear from him again.

Thus began Joseph Bates's exciting career—including his plunge from the mast into the ocean. For the next 21 years he devoted his life to the sea, never spending much time at his home port. His adventures were many and exciting, as he sailed the world over.

In 1810 he was kidnapped in Liverpool by a press gang and forced into the British Navy. By disregarding nationalities, Britain forced thousands of Americans into the British Navy during this time. When England and America went to war, Bates and his friends chose to become prisoners of war rather than fight against their own countrymen.

At that time Dartmoor Prison was known as "the abode of lost and forgotten men." It was to that most terrible of places that Bates and many others were sent. All the horrors that have been written about Dartmoor proved to be true. The eight months Bates spent there was a time of unspeakable privation and brutality.

Joseph was among the 260 prisoners released from Dartmoor on April 17, 1815. When he became aware of the date, he realized it had been exactly five years since the day he'd been kidnapped in Liverpool. He was assigned to the British ship *Mary Ann* for his journey home.

As they neared Newfoundland, the men on board began to talk about icebergs. A number of them, including Joseph, had seen icebergs in that area on previous voyages. They spoke to Captain Carr about the matter, but he refused to even consider the possibility. "I've made 15 voyages to Newfoundland," he jeered, "and never once have I seen any ice."

By 9:00 that night a strong wind was blowing. It became worse, but the captain refused to slow the ship, and it hurled along at high speed. Some of the Americans on board stationed themselves around the prow and sides of the ship, watching for danger. They were sure there must be icebergs nearby, for it became colder and colder. They were well aware that once an iceberg was actually seen in front of the ship, it would be too late to avoid it.

The men pleaded with the captain, who wasn't even on the bridge, to take in the sails. Not willing to admit his mistake, he refused to listen. In desperation one of the men shook his fist in the captain's face and shouted, "Sail is gonna be taken in either with or without your permission!"

Captain Carr knew he was outnumbered, and gave the order to strike the sails. For the rest of the night the ship bobbed peacefully up and down on the waves. At daybreak all on board were appalled to see huge icebergs all around them. Without comment the captain gave careful orders as they zigzagged their way out of the field of ice.

A few days after the iceberg incident some of the men realized they were off the coast of Maine. Many of the former prisoners were from the New England area, and they eagerly asked the captain where they were going to land. They didn't like what they heard. He wasn't going to stop. They would be set ashore at City Point, down in Virginia.

These men had been away from home for several years. They'd been imprisoned and mistreated. They weren't about to tolerate the nonsense of going all the way to Virginia when they could easily land in New England. So once again they defied the captain, taking command of the ship and landing it at New London, Connecticut. It didn't take long for the word to spread that a ship with released prisoners of war had just landed. Some of the men were reunited with their families that very same day.

As for Joseph, he booked passage on a ship going to Boston. Arriving there, he went immediately to the home of a good friend of his father's, who welcomed him with open arms. He was more than glad to lend Joseph enough money to get the necessary clothing to replace his tattered prison uniform and to pay the stagecoach fare to New Bedford.

A few days later the whole family went wild with joy when he appeared in the doorway of his home. The news spread quickly, and neighbors and friends kept dropping by to welcome him home. They all wanted to hear of his adventures, for he'd been away from home for six long years.

But it was within the family circle that evening that Joseph made his full report. He had asked his mother to invite his friend, Prudence Nye, to join them, and she sat by the fireside with the family, listening closely. Without really meaning to, he found himself telling the family of his trials and the brutal mistreatment he'd endured as a prisoner. Suddenly realizing the emotional effect around the family circle, he switched to a more cheerful narration of some of the lighter events of his experiences.

A full moon shone as Joseph walked Prudence to her home around midnight. As they talked, he realized that his fears of another man taking his place in her heart had been unfounded. At her gate he took her hand in his. "Prudence, I can't tell you how happy and thankful I am to be back," he said, "and to find you here to welcome me."

"Oh, Joseph, I'm so glad you're home again. I knew you'd come back." As is sometimes the case, each knew the thoughts of the other. But it was another two years before Joseph felt he was financially able to support a wife and asked her to marry him.

They were married on February 15, 1818, but marriage didn't end Joseph's love affair with the sea. He sailed on and on, being at home only for a few weeks at a time. His goal—and Prudence understood and accepted it—was to retire when he had saved $10,000, a fortune in those days.

Joseph's career at sea saw him advancing steadily, eventually achieving the rank of captain, then captain and co-owner of his own ship.

CHANGES ON BOARD

Over the years Joseph became more and more interested in religion, as well as a wide variety of reforms. Life on board ship had a way of emphasizing the evils of tobacco, hard liquor, beer and wine, and profane language, and one by one he eliminated them from his life. Later on he banished tea and coffee, and soon noticed his increased energy and feeling of well-being without them. He often quoted Sylvester Graham on the harmful effects of tea and coffee.

Captain Bates watched his men making preparations for the *Empress* to set sail from New Bedford. It was a three-masted schooner, and as half owner Bates was delighted with it. It was a fitting ship for his last voyage before retirement.

A couple of hours later the ship sailed out of the bay and into the Atlantic Ocean. As soon as things were well in hand, Captain Bates called his crew together. He laid out a set of rules that must have astonished this group of rough seamen.

First, said the captain, the members of the crew would address each other by their full Christian name. For instance, William Jones was to be William, not Bill or Willy. James Smith was to be James, not Jim or Jimmy. And so on. Neither would they use nicknames.

One might speculate whether Joseph Bates was ever called Joe, or Joey, or some other nickname. But with this account of his rule on names, it seems certain that he wasn't. It isn't known whether it was something instilled in him by his father and mother, or whether it was his own preference. A good guess would be that if anybody ever called him Joe, they did it only once!

Then he announced the second rule. "There will be no swearing during this voyage."

It can be imagined that most of the men stood open-mouthed at this, but one of the crewman, William Dunn, took issue and boldly announced, "I've always had that privilege, sir."

"Well," said Captain Bates, "you can't have it here." To make his point, he went on to quote the third commandment, and said that the Lord's name was not to be taken in vain on his ship.

Crewman Dunn couldn't give it up. "I can't help it, sir," he protested. "I'm very likely to swear before I even think of what I'm saying."

The captain assured him that proper discipline would be forthcoming if he forgot this rule.

As land faded from sight, the captain laid out a third unique rule: There would be no washing or mending of clothes on Sunday. Saturday afternoon, not Sunday, would be their free time, and they could wash and mend their clothes then. These chores were not to be done on Sunday. In addition, the men would appear every Sunday morning with clean clothes. Just because they were at sea was no excuse for dirty or tattered clothing. Furthermore, there would be no shore leaves on Sundays.

By this time it was too late to jump ship, and Captain Bates delivered his most stunning blow. "Gentlemen," he said, "there is no liquor on board, and it is strictly forbidden to bring it back from shore leave."

"And, by the way, every morning there will be a worship time, with church services on Sunday." When he finished his list of new rules, the captain knelt on the deck and committed his ship and his men to God.

It can be seen that Joseph Bates was a complex man—sometimes difficult to understand, but a man of sterling character.

After this voyage—which his men actually enjoyed, and asked to ship out with him again—Joseph Bates retired from the sea and turned his attention to religion and several progressive projects in which he was especially interested.

He was a reformer, ready for action in the great time of revolution in American history. Joseph Bates organized one of the first temperance societies in America. A man of many and varied interests, he was involved in several reform organizations.

PREACHING IN THE SOUTH

One afternoon as Bates worked in his orchard, a friend came by and asked if he was interested in going to a Millerite lecture that night. Bates accepted the invitation and was convicted of the truth of the speaker's words—that Jesus was coming in 1843 or 1844.

Making a special trip to Boston to learn about William Miller, Joseph met Joshua V. Himes, a great preacher in his own right, who was more than happy to share his knowledge of William Miller and his teachings. As stated in an earlier chapter, after years of Bible study Miller calculated that Jesus would return to earth about 1843 or 1844, and finally accepted God's call to tell others about his discoveries.

Other scholars kept studying Miller's findings, and they set the time of Christ's return to earth as October 22, 1844. Most Millerites accepted the date; however, William Miller himself accepted it only two or three weeks before the time.

This was exciting news to Joseph Bates, and he threw all his energies, as well as his money, into the work of spreading the good news that Jesus was coming soon. He now devoted his carefully accumulated fortune to preaching the Advent message.

As the Millerite Advent message was spread, Joseph Bates was burdened because no one seemed interested—or willing—to go south and preach the good news to the masters and their slaves. The more he thought about it, the more convinced he became that he should go. But he needed someone to travel with him. He hesitated to travel alone to such a volatile section of the country, but didn't know whom he could enlist to come with him on such a dangerous journey.

Ah! His old friend, H. S. Gurney, the singing blacksmith, would be just the man. Bates lost no time in making a visit to the blacksmith shop and related his burden for someone to take the message to the South.

Mr. Gurney paused in his work. "My friend," he said, "if the Lord has laid the burden on your heart, you should be the one to go."

"Yes, I'd like to do just that," Bates agreed. "But given the political climate, I'd rather not go alone. Would you be willing to go with me?"

Being a man of common sense, Gurney well knew there was a very real danger that the Southerners would suspect them of being abolitionists and lynch them on the spot. He wanted a few days to think it over, and Bates was glad for even this consideration.

True to his word, Gurney gave careful thought to the matter. A few days later he sent word to Bates that he'd go with him in spite of the danger.

The two friends traveled down to Maryland, crossing over Chesapeake Bay to Kent Island, where Bates had been shipwrecked more than 25 years before. He recognized the area as the place where he had run aground. Soon they came to a small town that looked like a good place to begin their meetings. The town boasted two meetinghouses, and the men asked permission to hold services in one of them. Their request was refused by the trustees of both places.

Then the tavern keeper, who always kept abreast of what was going on in town, came to Captain Bates and asked, "Did you say your name was Bates?"

"That's right; Joseph Bates."

"Were you shipwrecked near here many years ago?"

Bates said yes, that his ship had run aground near there, but wondered how this man knew about it.

The tavern keeper cleared up the mystery. "Mr. Bates, you came to my father's house that night and stayed several hours. I was only about 10 years old at that time, but I well remember your being there."

On the strength of that long-ago meeting, he invited Bates and Gurney to hold their meeting in his tavern hall, and it was announced for the following afternoon. The hall was well filled when Mr. Gurney opened the service with singing, his rich voice inspiring those who listened.

For the next five days Bates and Gurney held meetings in the tavern hall, with a capacity attendance each day. On the last day some of the town rowdies decided Bates and Gurney probably *were* abolitionists, and hatched a plan to cause a riot that would break up the service.

Hearing of this threat, Bates went right on with his sermon. The troublemakers didn't show up, but just as Bates finished, one of the men who'd refused the use of his building began to shout obscenities about the speaker and his message. "I can put this whole thing down in 10 minutes," he loudly proclaimed.

With a welcoming smile, Joseph Bates told him, "Brother, you are welcome to come forward and state your claim."

Coming to the speaker's stand, he began his statement. However, he succeeded only in establishing the certainty that he knew nothing about the subject. Suddenly he shook his fist at Bates and yelled, "We're gonna ride you outta town on a rail!"

"We're quite ready for that," Bates calmly replied. "And by the way, if you'd put a saddle on it, we'd much rather ride than walk."

The crowd appreciated this quick and witty comeback, but then Bates continued. "You mustn't think that we have come 600 miles through ice and snow, at our own expense, to give this good news to you without first sitting down and counting the cost. And now, if the Lord has no more for us to do, we had as [soon] lie at the bottom of Chesapeake Bay as anywhere else until the Lord comes. But if He has any more work for us to do, you can't touch us!"

The situation was smoothed over, apologies were given, and they were invited to come back again.

In Chester, Maryland, they found a meeting place where they could speak to both slaves and their owners. Bates asked Gurney to open the meeting with a song they both had come to love. This was a new song to them, and it somehow expressed their feelings as they followed God's direction in spreading the joyful news of Christ's soon coming. Once again Gurney lifted up his voice and sang:

"I'm a pilgrim, and I'm a stranger;
I can tarry, I can tarry but a night;
Do not detain me, for I am going to where the fountains are ever flowing.
I'm a pilgrim, and I'm a stranger;
I can tarry, I can tarry but a night."

As the last notes died away, hearts were touched, and both slaves and masters listened intently as Elder Bates presented the message. All around the back of the room stood scores of slaves, drinking in all that was said. When the meeting was over, they waited patiently as the White people left; then Bates and Gurney spoke with them personally.

Bates asked the slaves, "Could you hear what was said? Did you believe it?"

"Oh, yes, we could hear; we could understand, and we believe it all. And we want some of those papers you were handin' out to the masters."

"But can you read the papers?"

"No," they said, "but young missus or massa's son will read 'em for us." So the truth-filled papers were left with them.

One of the slaves, an old, white-haired gentleman, came to Heman Gurney afterward and asked for a copy of that song he had sung. Since it was the only copy he had, Gurney had to tell the old man that he was sorry but that he couldn't part with it. Then the man offered him 25 cents for a copy of the song he had heard that night—"I'm a Pilgrim, and I'm a Stranger." It's likely that was all the money he had in the world, and there's no way of knowing how long it had taken him to save it.

He probably felt that his life story was told right there in the song. He had been owned by another person all of his life, and now he had the "blessed hope" of Jesus' soon coming. Now he knew that there was something better in store for him; he was going to where the fountains were ever flowing. He stood before Gurney, his face pleading for the words to the song he already loved.

Gurney's heart was touched by the old man's earnestness. From somewhere a stub of pencil and a scrap of paper were produced, and Gurney copied it out for him. The man went away with a huge smile on his face, delighted to have a copy of this wonderful song that spoke so strongly to his heart. And no doubt he went away with his 25 cents as well!

Those who truly believed in the validity of October 22, 1844, as the date for Christ's return made every preparation to meet Him. But October 22 came and went, and Christ didn't appear. The next day found Captain Bates deeply embarrassed as well as gravely disappointed. He'd left his small crop of potatoes in the ground to testify to his faith in Jesus' coming. His neighbors had offered to buy them, but he felt he'd be cheating them, for he was sure that they'd never have the opportunity to use them. As a highly respected member of the community, he had urged his neighbors to prepare for the Second Coming. Now they taunted him in the streets until he wished the ground would open up and swallow him.

In addition, the believers could hardly contain their grief. Bates later said: "The effect of this disappointment can be realized only by those who experienced it."

WORSHIPPING ON THE SEVENTH DAY

One morning as Captain Bates opened his mail, he found a little paper entitled *The Hope of Israel*. In it was an article by T. M. Preble in which he pointed out the necessity of keeping the seventh-day Sabbath. Bates didn't agree, but took his Bible and looked up the texts mentioned in the article. The more he studied, the more uneasy he became. It really didn't seem possible that he, and most others, had been worshipping on a day not set aside by God. He thought about the matter for several days.

Questions flooded his mind: *Should he keep the seventh day? How would Prudence feel about this? What would his friends think of him? How would he make a living?*

But once he decided that the seventh-day Sabbath was the only one taught in the Bible, the questions fell away. They were no longer of prime importance. He must do what God had asked him to do.

Captain Bates heard about a group of Advent believers in Washington, New Hampshire, who were keeping the seventh-day Sabbath. Before making a drastic announcement that would change his life, Bates determined to visit the place and be sure of his ground.

So it was that in the spring of 1845, Captain Bates took the train as far up through New England as it went, then changed to the stagecoach, which took him to the town of Hillsboro. He was given directions to the home of Frederick Wheeler, pastor of the Washington, New Hampshire, church. He knocked on the door at 10:00 at night.

Apologizing for the lateness of the hour, Bates said it was most important that he talk with the pastor. Upon learning that Bates wanted to hear about the Sabbath, Wheeler quickly invited him to come in.

"I want to know every argument there is in the Bible in favor of the seventh-day Sabbath," Bates began. "I'm convinced it's the only day of rest taught in the Scriptures, but hardly anybody knows about it. Brother Wheeler, this is a subject that must be broadcast everywhere!"

The two men studied the Bible and talked until morning. Bates asked questions and took notes, becoming more convinced than ever of the truth of the Sabbath. Wheeler gave him a copy of Preble's tract on the Sabbath. As the sun rose over the hills of New Hampshire, it shone through the sparkling window on two figures as they knelt on the braided rug and committed their lives to preaching the Sabbath truth.

"Brother Bates," as he was introduced to the family, was welcomed warmly to the Wheeler breakfast table, and then joined them in prayers. Wheeler hitched up Old Billy to the buggy, and the two men drove 12 miles to the home of Cyrus Farnsworth. It was a warm day, and they sat under the maple trees in the front yard as Wheeler and Farnsworth gave their guest a crash course on everything they had learned about the Sabbath.

This experience, along with reading Preble's tract, confirmed for Bates the continuing validity of the fourth commandment. His mission accomplished, he said his farewells and headed back to Hillsboro, where he would catch the stage. The journey home would take about three days, and he had a lot to think about as he traveled the 160 miles by stagecoach and train. He was convinced that everything he had studied with the Washington Sabbathkeepers was substantiated by the Bible. Being an honest man, he knew and accepted truth when he saw it.

Walking home from the train depot, Captain Bates met his neighbor, James Madison Monroe Hall, on the wooden bridge between New Bedford and Fairhaven. Hall cheerfully greeted him with "What's the good news, Captain Bates?"

"The good news is that the seventh day is the Sabbath" was Bates's eager reply.

After a short conversation on the bridge, Bates made arrangements to present the matter to Hall and the other Advent believers. By the next weekend Mr. Hall was keeping the Sabbath, and his wife followed by the next Sabbath. As an indication of his high regard for the retired sea captain, he later named his newborn son Joseph Bates Hall.

Joseph Bates played a major role in the adoption of the seventh-day Sabbath by a large segment of the disappointed Adventists. He had a real burden to find the disappointed believers and teach them about the Sabbath. After the Disappointment, Bates joined the group that met at Hiram Edson's home in Port Gibson, New York, to study the Bible further. It soon became apparent to the group that they had the time right but the event wrong. They came to see that the event was not the coming of Christ but the beginning of the investigative judgment. By then Joseph Bates had been keeping the Sabbath for about a year, and he shared his paper on the Sabbath with the group. Edson had already been thinking of the matter, though not until that time did he see that it held real importance. He and several others in the group accepted the good news of the Sabbath.

In 1848 six conferences were held dealing with the Sabbath question in particular. At most of the sessions Bates lectured on the Sabbath, and James White—who with his wife, Ellen, had accepted the Sabbath in 1847—spoke on the three angels' messages, which included the sanctuary and the Spirit of prophecy.

So many came to the conference of Sabbathkeepers at the home of David Arnold in Volney, New York, that the meeting had to be moved to the barn in order to accommodate everyone. At the close of that conference Bates and the Whites went on to Port Gibson, New York, where another conference was held at the home of Hiram Edson, again in a barn. Hoping to spend the Sabbath in New York City, Elder and Mrs. White, along with Captain Bates, left Port Gibson immediately after the conference closed. Their transportation would be a packet boat on the Erie Canal.

As the canal boat came near the dock, they began to gather up their bags. Suddenly they realized that the boat wasn't going to stop; it was just swinging in near the dock but not actually stopping. Elder White picked up his diminutive wife and with a mighty leap landed on the deck. Bates didn't have the same good fortune. He happened to be holding the fare for the three of them, and he stood on the dock, yelling to the captain, "Here! Here, take your pay!"

As the boat moved off into the canal without him, he took a mighty leap forward to get aboard. Unfortunately, his foot hit the edge of the boat, and he tumbled backward into the dirty water. The small crowd on the deck gasped as he went under. Bates surfaced and began to tread water. He still had his pocketbook in one hand and the dollar bill in the other. Then his hat fell off. In saving his hat, he lost the dollar bill—but he held fast to his pocketbook.

The boat stopped long enough for him to be plucked from the muddy canal water. Torn between the humor of the situation and pity for the poor man, who, of course, was soaked through and through, the passengers reached out to Bates and pulled him aboard. Fortunately the day was warm, and Bates's clothes dried out somewhat. The little party was able to disembark a few stops later at Centerport, where they made their way to the home of Brother Harris. There Bates was able to get his clothes dried and pressed, and the next day they continued on their journey.

THE LORD *DID* PROVIDE

One of Joseph Bates's favorite sayings was "The Lord will provide." By 1846 Bates had used his entire fortune in proclaiming the soon coming of Christ. When he traveled, money for his fare usually came to him just in the nick of time, sometimes even from total strangers. The Lord did indeed provide.

No telling of Bates's experiences would be complete without the story of the four pounds of flour. Early in 1846 he felt called of God to write a tract on the Sabbath. One morning as he sat at his desk writing, his wife, Prudy, as he called her, came in to tell him that she didn't have enough flour to finish the baking. He asked how much she needed, and she guessed about four pounds.

At the store Joseph bought the four pounds of flour and a few other small things she'd added to the list. Back at home he left them on the kitchen table and went back to his writing.

In a few minutes Prudy came into his study. "Joseph," she asked, "where did this flour come from?"

He must have heard something amiss in her voice, for he asked, "Isn't that enough? You said you needed four pounds."

She pressed him further. "Where did you get the flour?"

"Well, Prudy, I bought it. Isn't that the amount you wanted?"

Her reply became famous. "Yes; but have *you*, Captain Bates, a man who has sailed vessels out of New Bedford to all parts of the world, gone out and bought *four* pounds of flour?"

Then he had to admit that he'd spent his last cent on earth for those few items. This came as a real blow to Prudy. Of course, she knew and approved of his generous spending for the cause of God. But to think they had nothing left!

Tears flowing, she sobbed, "What are we going to do?"

The captain rose from his chair with all the dignity of his rank. "I am going to write a book and spread the Sabbath truth to all the world."

She wanted to know, of course, what they were going to live on. With a gentle smile he reassured her, "The Lord will provide."

Throwing her apron over her eyes, she ran from the room. "Oh, yes," she sobbed, "the Lord will provide. The Lord will provide. That's what you always say."

About a half hour later Bates was impressed that there was an important letter waiting for him at the post office. Arriving there, he found that indeed there was a letter, but he had to admit to his friend, Mr. Drew, the postmaster, that he didn't have the five cents to pay its postage.

"Oh, go ahead and take the letter, Mr. Bates. Pay the postage later." But there was no "Buy now, pay later" for Joseph Bates.

"Mr. Drew," he countered, "please open the letter for me. If there is money in it, take the cost of the postage out before you give it to me."

Inside the envelope was a $10 bill. The sender explained that the Lord had so impressed him that Bates was in need of money that he sent it post haste. In fact, he sent it in such haste that he forgot to pay the postage. Those were the days when the sender usually paid the postage, but if he didn't, then the receiver had to pay it.

With a happy heart and thanks to his Lord, Bates went out and bought a barrel of flour for $4, plus potatoes, sugar, and other items. He told the deliveryman that his wife probably would say it didn't belong there, but to leave it on the front porch anyway. Then he went to the printshop and arranged for the printing of his as-yet-unwritten pamphlet. He ordered 1,000 copies, telling the printer that he would pay in full before taking delivery. He had no money for the print job, but he knew that the Lord would provide.

At home he found a very excited Prudy who demanded to know where the provisions had come from. We can imagine his answer: "The Lord sent them."

And her reply was the standard one: "Yes, yes, the Lord sent them. That's what you always say."

With a big smile he handed her the letter. She read it and then retired for another good cry, but this time in a very different frame of mind.

Although Mrs. Bates supported her husband's work, she herself hadn't yet accepted the Sabbath. She didn't just follow him blindly, but studied for herself for five years—until 1850—when she also became a Sabbathkeeper. Local legend has it that during this time Joseph drove Prudy to her church on Sunday but declined to attend services with her on this "unsanctified" day.

It is to our loss that Bates's *Autobiography* and his other writings mention very little about Prudence and their five children. One son died in infancy while his father was away at sea. Their other son, who inherited his father's love of the seafaring life, was lost at sea at the age of 35. Their three daughters survived them.

The church paper, the *Review and Herald,* carried three letters from Prudence Bates in the 1850s. They give a little glimpse into her own solid character and her commitment to God. Here are just a few sentences from December 1851:

"I feel an increasing desire to be filled with all the fullness of God, and the more I strive for this the more I see my own unworthiness.

Sometimes I feel almost discouraged, and were it not that the cloud breaks away and a sunbeam of glory illumines my pathway . . . I should despair."

She mentioned how unworthy she felt, but how precious Jesus was to her, and how she loved the Sabbath. Her husband wasn't the only one with a sterling character.

In August the printer sent word to Bates that the pamphlets were ready. As money had come to him Bates had paid part of the cost, but quite a sum was still due. True to form, Bates absolutely would not take delivery of the papers until he could pay for them, and he hurried over to the printshop to explain. When he got there, the printer told him they were all paid for. Once he recovered his power of speech, he asked who had paid for them.

"I don't know, Mr. Bates. He was a stranger to me."

Joseph Bates never found out who paid for the pamphlets, but the rest of his life he remained grateful to the unknown person.

WHEN JOSEPH MET ELLEN

Joseph Bates first met Ellen Harmon about 1845, and again in 1847. Neither was particularly impressed with the other. Skeptical and suspicious of any supernatural manifestations, he found it difficult to accept her experience as being from the Lord, but he couldn't find any fault in her life or in her testimony. However, he was, as he said, "alarmed and tried exceedingly."

For her part, she found Bates to be a kindly father figure. (He was more than 30 years older than she.) She was puzzled, however, that such a genuine Christian should emphasize the fourth commandment so strongly. Didn't he know there were nine other commandments?

Then in November 1847 Bates witnessed her in vision as she was shown stars and planets. During the vision—unknown to Ellen herself—she spoke of what she was seeing and gave a description of rosy-tinted belts around one of the planets, adding that she saw four moons.

"Oh," exclaimed Captain Bates, "she's looking at Jupiter!" A bit later she described seeing seven moons.

Again Bates exclaimed, "She's describing Saturn!"

As a sailor Bates knew a good deal about the heavenly bodies. By the time the vision was over and she had described Uranus, with its six moons, and the "opening heavens" in a way that Bates said far surpassed any account he'd ever read, he was beginning to change his mind about Ellen's visions.

When she came out of the vision, he asked her if she had ever studied astronomy.

"No," she said. "I don't remember ever looking into an astronomy book."

His happy conviction was "This is of the Lord."

WESTWARD HO!

Joseph had retired from his roaming of the seas. Now he roamed over the land, eager to tell everyone about the soon return of Jesus and about the Sabbath. One morning Prudy walked into their bedroom and saw her husband packing his bag—again. She almost cried.

When he told her he was going west, Prudy thought he meant he was going to California. No, no, he explained. He was going to Michigan, and maybe Ohio and Indiana, to find the "lost sheep." He felt that he must find as many former Advent believers as he could and tell them about the Sabbath.

That made her feel somewhat better, but she truly wished he wouldn't go away again. After all, he was getting older, and he needed to stay at home. But off he went on his errands for the Lord.

He went first to Indiana and held meetings in South Bend. One night he dreamed that he was on a stagecoach, going northeast to an unknown village. When he woke in the morning, he felt he must go on without delay. Taking passage on the first stage out of South Bend, he felt certain he'd recognize the town when he came to it. At every town he got out, looked around, and decided that that wasn't the place. Then he'd pay the fare to the next stop and repeat the procedure. The stage driver must have wondered at his passenger's strange behavior. But when Bates jumped out of the stage at Jackson, Michigan, he knew it was the place he'd seen in his dream.

Walking up the street to a boardinghouse, he asked the owner, "Are there any Advent believers in this town?"

"Why, yes, there are. About 20 of them meet here every Sunday." This was what he was looking for. The believers were still looking for Jesus to come, but they hadn't heard about the Sabbath. They were still worshipping on Sunday.

On up the street, Bates came to a blacksmith shop. He went in and hung up his chart, which was always with him. Introducing himself to Dan Palmer, the blacksmith, he proceeded to tell him of the seventh-day Sabbath, and all the other truths that were so dear to him.

As a result, Palmer invited him to meet with the group on Sunday. Before Bates left town, a good-sized group of Advent believers were keeping the Sabbath.

THE MOST HONEST MAN IN TOWN

Two years later on a return trip to Jackson, Bates went to see his friend Dan Palmer, who was delighted to see him again. In fact, he had been studying with another group, and they were ready for baptism. This, of course, was music to Bates's ears.

Just before his departure from Jackson, Bates had another dream. In this one he was headed west from Jackson. He was told in the dream that he must stop and work in Battle Creek, Michigan. The next morning he asked Palmer if he knew of a town called Battle Creek.

"Oh, sure. It's about 40 miles up the railroad."

"Are there any Advent believers there?"

"Not a one that I know of."

"Well, Dan, I was shown last night in a dream that that is to be my next place of labor."

The early-morning mail train got him to Battle Creek just about breakfast time. Not knowing exactly how to go about his business there, he thought of the post office. He was looking for an honest person, and the postmaster would surely know where to direct him.

At the post office Bates asked for the name and address of the most honest man in town. He was immediately directed to the home of David Hewitt. Bates felt that an honest man would readily accept the Advent message.

David Hewitt opened the door to his knock. Bates was completely frank with him:

"I've been directed to you as the most honest man in town. If this is so, I have some important truth to present to you."

"Come on in" was the easy invitation. "We're just about to have breakfast. Come and eat with us, and then we'll talk."

As they ate and chatted, Hewitt was taking measure of the stranger who sat at his table. He discerned an honest, forthright man, an earnest Christian. After breakfast he invited Captain Bates to conduct their morning worship, which he was happy to do. Afterward Hewitt said, "Now we'll hear what you have to tell us."

After a day together in Bible study with Joseph Bates, the "most honest man in town" and his wife accepted the Sabbath message and became the first converts in Battle Creek.

THE MOVE TO MICHIGAN

More and more, Bates was drawn to "the West," especially to Michigan, and more especially to Monterey. He felt that tent efforts should be made in the west. It seemed to him that the angels of God were preparing minds there to receive the truth. He felt that it was of great importance that the servants of God move where He opened the way.

For these and other reasons, in May 1858 Joseph Bates decided to move to Michigan. Prudence wasn't altogether happy about the move, for she'd lived in Fairhaven all her life. But she went where Joseph wanted to go. And that was not to Battle Creek, but to Monterey. The move didn't mean that Bates had retired from the Lord's work. He just relocated his headquarters, though perhaps his trips were less lengthy than before.

James White urged Bates that his age should excuse him from so much travel and public speaking. But Bates replied, "I still want to go along beside you, [even] if I can't do a great deal." Bates said he was reminded of a farmer who had a horse so old it was left in the stable when the others were taken out to plow. The man heard a tremendous noise at the stable, and upon investigation found the horse kicking to get out. So they put a collar on him and hitched him by the side of the others. He spent his remaining days walking beside the other horses, perfectly contented. So it was with Brother Bates. If he couldn't work, he asked the brethren to "let me have a collar on and walk by the side of the rest."

Although he never said much about his healthful living patterns, over the years Joseph Bates had eliminated one harmful habit after another. As a result he enjoyed a state of health that could be envied. The year before he died he attended a health reform rally in the old Battle Creek church. As the subject was discussed, someone asked, "Where's Elder Bates? He's the one we need to hear from on this subject."

Elder Bates was sitting toward the back of the church. As they called him to come to the front, this dear old gentleman, then 79 years old and still ramrod straight, walked briskly to the platform to tell what healthful living habits had done for him. He recalled his experience of the past, and the result of dropping one bad habit after another until he reached the point of total abstinence of everything he knew to be harmful. He said he was entirely free from aches and pains.

J. O. Corliss, who was present at the meeting, gave this testimony: Elder Bates "stood straight as a marble shaft, and tripped about as lightly as a boy. The audience was so electrified by the aged man's eloquence that for a moment only deep 'amens' were to be heard."

J. N. Andrews was then called upon for his part in the program, which seems to have been a lecture on the benefits of health reform. As he stepped to the pulpit, his first words were: "What shall the man do who comes after the king?" After a few long seconds of reflection he went on with his talk.

It was said that Bates's testimony went a long way toward putting the cause of health reform in its rightful place.

Two years after the death of his beloved Prudy, Joseph Bates was called to his rest on March 19, 1872. He left a large gap in the work of the Lord and in the lives of whose who knew and loved him. At the Michigan Conference meeting held in the fall of that same year, a resolution of sorrow was passed. It read, "While we deeply mourn our loss, we will remember his counsels, imitate his virtues, and endeavor to meet him in the kingdom of God."

"He will see his Lord a-coming."

Rachel Harris Oakes Preston

She Stood Up for the Sabbath

"It's a little chilly out this morning, Mother; better wear your wool wrap," Delight Oakes called over her shoulder as she stepped outside.

"OK, I've got it and my pamphlets." Rachel tightened her grip on the thin tracts as a cool March breeze threatened to take them from her hand. Not that handing them out had done much good since she moved to Washington, New Hampshire, a few months ago. It seemed this group was more engrossed with the soon return of the Lord than with following the fourth commandment. *Their eyes were so fixed on the sky that they couldn't seem to keep track of how many times the sun rises and sets in a week!*

She had first heard about worshipping on Saturday when she lived in Vernon, New York. At the time she was attending the Methodist church, but it was from the local Seventh Day Baptist church that she first was introduced to the Sabbath as Saturday.

"I am not sure how eager these members are to change their day of worship, Mother."

"I know, but one never knows when an opportunity might present itself."

During the past few months there had been a twist of the conversation here and there, but often it seemed the subject held no interest. Rachel had even used her schoolteacher's voice, but learned adults were not always willing students. When she first became convicted of the day, she tried to share it with her Methodist pastor, but he was not convinced. In the 1830s it was an act of bravery for a woman to stand up to her pastor. He spent as much time trying to keep her as a member as she spent trying to change his day of worship.

Delight had followed in her mother's career footsteps and accepted the position as the local schoolteacher; and being a widow, Rachel had joined her in her new home.

The parishioners bustled into the Christian church, taking their seats in their family pews. Today the presiding elder would be Frederick Wheeler, the Methodist circuit preacher, who had come into town from Hillsboro and was there that day to conduct the communion service. Elder Wheeler had accepted the Advent message, making him a welcome speaker to this congregation, who eagerly awaited the Second Coming.

Frederick stood to preach and scanned the group of parishioners; it was encouraging to see many familiar and receptive faces, but his eyes lingered for a moment on the middle-aged woman sitting with the new schoolteacher. This was someone he had not seen before. She was listening so intently with her bright eyes trained on him that he had to clear his throat so he could take a moment to focus his thoughts back on the prepared words. Confidently he declared, "All who confess communion with Christ in such a service as this should be ready to obey and keep God's commandments in all things."

That did it! Rachel all but jumped to her feet in protest. *How could he stand up there on Sunday and lecture them about keeping all the commandments?* The thought made her blood boil. Her whole body suddenly felt very warm, and she struggled to free herself from her wrap.

"Mother, please calm down," Delight whispered out of the side of her mouth.

"It is suddenly very warm in here, and I am wearing this wool wrap!" she whispered through tight lips, looking pointedly at her daughter.

After the service Rachel sought out Elder Wheeler. Her gaze leveled at him. "You remember, Elder Wheeler, that you said everyone who confesses Christ should obey all the commandments of God?"

"Yes."

"I came near getting up in the meeting right then and saying something." She squared her shoulders.

"What did you have in mind to say?" He held her gaze.

"I wanted to tell you that you had better set that communion table back and put the cloth over it until you begin to keep the commandments of God!" came her resounding reply.

Elder Wheeler sat back, astonished. He was grateful that she had not said this in front of the congregation. *Am I being disobedient to God and His commandments?* It was a sobering thought. He had heard that a new member was handing out pamphlets about the seventh-day Sabbath, but he had not given the idea much thought. Now in one sentence this woman had preached an entire sermon to his ears. He was a minister *and yet* was not observing all the commandments, specifically the fourth. It shook him to the core.

Rachel could see he was processing this information, so she kept uncharacteristically quiet and watched him think through what she had said.

Years later Elder Wheeler recounts that those words cut him deeper than any that had ever been spoken to him.

◆ ◆ ◆

Rachel Delight Harris was born in 1809 in Vernon, Vermont. She was married at an early age to Amory Oakes and welcomed their daughter, Delight, a year later, around 1825. When she was 17, she joined the Methodist Church.

Sometime later Amory, Rachel, and Delight moved to Verona, New York. It was there that Rachel first learned of the seventh-day Sabbath. She was in her mid-20s, and once convicted, Rachel became a steadfast believer. Amory didn't accept the message of the Sabbath, and he and their Methodist minister were not supportive of her decision at all. Rachel took a brave stance, holding firm to her beliefs and opposing her husband, a trait not commonly found in wives at that time. It must not have been easy, but she could take comfort in her dedication to the Lord's Word. It was then that she joined the Seventh Day Baptist church of Verona, New York.

Amory died while the family was living in New York. When Delight was 18, she secured a teaching position in Washington, New Hampshire. Her widowed mother came to live with her and brought with her the message of the seventh-day Sabbath.

The Christian church there in New Hampshire was on fire for the Advent! It was 1843, and the foremost thought on every Christian's mind was the second coming of Jesus Christ! Rachel was still strongly convicted of her understanding of the fourth commandment and didn't hesitate to speak up about it. She made a marked effort to share her Seventh Day Baptist literature with this group, but they were so preoccupied with preparing for the Lord's return that her message was often set aside. But this was not a woman to be cast off, and she stayed true to her cause.

Elder Wheeler began that day in March 1844 without any clue that his after-church conversation with the outspoken member of the congregation would forever change the course of his life.

Once Rachel put the thought of the seventh-day Sabbath into Elder Wheeler's head, he couldn't shake it. He studied and pondered, and quickly concluded that she was correct! He too began to observe and preach that the seventh day was the Sabbath. History notes that he was the first pastor of the Seventh-day Adventists.

The example of Rachel and Pastor Wheeler started to gain attention from the members of that congregation, specifically from a member named William Farnsworth. Later that year he publicly declared that he would keep the Sabbath on the seventh day. As it does with many actions, it takes one or two to set an example, and soon others follow. And others did, creating the first church of Seventh-day Adventists.

One of those early adopters of the seventh-day Sabbath and the Advent

THE HOPEFUL **RACHEL HARRIS OAKES PRESTON**

message was William's brother, Cyrus Farnsworth. Delight caught his eye, and the two were married in June of 1847. They had four children.

Rachel took a little more time to accept the Advent message. She studied alongside her fellow church members, and eventually she came to share their same beliefs. Around 1856 she married Nathan T. Preston. From the church records it appears that he may have been in the ministry. The church's logbook shows that the parsonage was rented for a year to Mr. Preston in 1856. The Prestons moved back to Vernon, Vermont, and remained there until their deaths, Rachel in 1868 and Nathan in 1871.

One may never know the influence of even just one brave comment spoken from conviction; it may change someone's life, and in turn many more lives, forever. On Rachel's grave marker, the following tribute is inscribed:

> "Rachel Preston
> was used of God
> in bringing the
> truth of the Sabbath
> to the Adventist church
> in Washington, N.H.,
> which became the first
> Seventh-day Adventist
> Church in America."

James White

"You Will See Your Lord A-Coming"

Every seat was taken. People crowded into the aisles and onto the platform. The meetinghouse at Litchfield Plains was crammed with almost 1,000 people who had come to hear the young preacher tell about the soon return of Christ. With everybody talking at once, a joyful murmur filled the room.

To quiet them and get their attention, James White started what would become a standard practice for him. As he walked down the aisle toward the platform, he began to sing one of the new Advent hymns, thumping out the rhythm on the back of his Bible. One of his favorites, and the one he sang that night, was "You Will See Your Lord A-Coming"—a song written as the Advent believers anticipated seeing their Savior on October 22, 1844.

The first verse of the hymn is given here, with a slight adjustment in the words as it is now used—hymn number 438 in the 1985 *SDA Hymnal:*

> "You will see your Lord a-coming, you will see your Lord a-coming, you will see your Lord a-coming, in a few more days;
> Hear the band of music, hear the band of music, hear the band of music,
> Which is sounding through the air."

More than 30 years later, when James White was considerably older, with his beard and hair gone white, someone who heard him sing reported that his voice was still clear and silvery. It's easy to understand how the talking and shuffling in the house in Litchfield Plains quieted as the audience turned their attention to him.

As a matter of fact, James White came from a musical family. His father not only was a farmer and a shoemaker but also gave voice lessons. Singing was a gift in the White family. On one occasion when James, his father, and two sisters were traveling to a conference, they used their gift in an unusual way.

In those days most of the travel was done by horse and buggy, and that was the mode the White family used on this trip. Darkness fell before they reached their destination, and it began to rain, so they stopped for the night at a country inn. Of course, there were no electric lights, TV, radios, or video games—no entertainment for the long hours before bedtime. The evening stretched out before them as long and boring. But the Whites were a resourceful group, and they decided to just go into the big main room of the inn and sing some of the old hymns. It was an evening much like one they would have had at home.

The singing was so inviting that other guests, as well as the manager's family, drifted into the room, until there was quite a gathering. A fire burning in the fireplace made it a relaxing and cozy setting. As the White family finished one song, someone would request another one, and so the evening passed very pleasantly for everyone.

The next morning when Father White went to pay the bill, the manager told him there was no bill to pay. The innkeeper and his guests had been well paid by the evening of singing. Furthermore, the Whites were welcome to give a repeat performance any time they were in that vicinity. Is it any wonder that James was able to use his talent to such good effect with the crowd in Litchfield Plains!

James White was right in the middle of nine children—four were older, four were younger. A deacon in the local church, his father was a firm believer in the Scriptures, and didn't hesitate to follow wherever new light took him. Deacon John provided well for his family, both spiritually and economically. Although the physical labor was hard, the White family was content on their hillside farm. Not only was Deacon John a farmer, but he also was a shoemaker, a trade that all his boys learned along with him. He successfully taught his children the value of an honest day's work, as well as the value of honesty before God.

In the grip of an unyielding fever, relentless seizures had wracked the small body of 2-year-old James, and he lay deathly ill for many weeks. His mother anxiously watched over him, not knowing from one hour to the next whether he would live or die.

But live he did, though unfortunately, after he recovered, his eyes seemed to be permanently crossed. When he was 7, he went to school with his brothers and sisters, but his school experience didn't last long. As he tried to read, the letters all ran together, and he couldn't make sense of them. It was no use. Without reading, school was an unattainable dream.

Farm children were needed at home during the summer, so school was held for a few months during the winter. Because of the short school term, it was difficult for even the best of students to get a good education, and for a boy who couldn't see well enough to learn to read, it was impossible. James was forced to accept the probability that he would go through life illiterate.

Many years later James's brother John described the school they attended. "Every winter we would get over in old Webster as far as 'booby'—then go home and work it all out of body and brain. And next winter, repeat the farce."

James couldn't go to school, but he could be his father's right-hand man on the farm. With all the hard work, he grew strong and tall—six feet tall. Then in his late teens—a miracle occurred. His eyes returned to normal. He was no longer cross-eyed! Now that his eyes were well and he could read, he was determined to get an education.

At the age of 19 he presented his tall, gangly self to the teacher. "I'm sorry, James," he said, "but you'll have to start at the beginning."

Yes, right along with the younger children. So the eager young man folded his long legs onto the child-sized bench and started to school.

By diligent hard work for the 12 weeks school was in session, James learned in great leaps and bounds. At the end of the term, his teacher/mentor felt he was well able to teach younger children and gave him a certificate that authorized him to teach in the "common branches." Certificate in possession, he applied for, and received, a teaching position for the next winter.

James White's formal schooling amounted to 41 weeks—12 weeks in the primary school and 29 weeks in various schools of higher learning. However, he was so faithful in his schoolwork that the headmaster at the Methodist school in Redfield told him that one more semester would entitle him to enroll in college. Faithfully he saved his money; his aim was to go on to higher education. He would have been devastated had he known that his formal education was already over.

At home his mother mentioned that a Brother Oakes, from Boston, had been holding meetings at the schoolhouse. He was proving from the Bible that Jesus was coming back to earth very soon, and some people in their area believed what the man was teaching. James had heard of the Millerite teaching, but thought William Miller was a fanatic on the subject. For every objection James raised, his mother had an answer. At last, just to please her, he agreed to attend the meetings. He would see for himself what the Scriptures actually taught. As others before him, he was soon convinced that God Himself was leading this Advent movement.

Although he'd been baptized into the Christian Church at the age of 15, James wasn't all that interested in religion. He had an education to concentrate on. Nevertheless, as he attended Brother Oakes's meetings, God seemed to be convicting him that it was his duty to help warn people that Jesus was coming soon. He begged the Lord to remove this burden. But the idea—almost a voice—became ever stronger.

Visit your students, it said. *Visit your students*.

Finally giving up the struggle, he capitulated and listened to the voice of God. He didn't quite understand the great peace that flooded his heart.

The next day he went to visit some of his former students in Troy. James loved children and was loved and respected by them in return, so it's no surprise that he was given a warm welcome into the first home he visited. The teacher had come to visit and to pray for his students and their families! This was a momentous day, and the mother sent her children up and down the road to invite everyone they saw to come and hear the schoolmaster pray for them.

Within a half hour 25 people had crowded into the house. They sat on the chairs and the floor, and some stood leaning against the wall. "How many of you are Christians?" James asked. Not one of them. He spoke to them about what it means to follow Jesus and to be ready for His return. Then he prayed with them.

In just a few days he had found all his former students and prayed with them. Now he could get on with his studies. Returning to the academy, he found to his dismay that he still couldn't concentrate on his school work.

Go and preach! was the conviction that now came to him. James White was no match for the God of heaven, and after days of grappling with the problem, he finally gave his heart completely to Jesus. Once he committed his life fully to Christ, he never looked back.

TRAVELING PREACHER

He would go and preach. As he mapped out his itinerary, he decided he would preach one or two nights in each place. Three sermons would be enough, and he'd repeat them in each new place. And so with a few pieces of Advent literature, a chart, and three sermons, the young James White was ready to go.

Well, almost ready to go.

There *was* one small problem. He had no horse, no saddle, and no money. His father came to the rescue by letting him use his horse for the winter. The minister gave him a shabby old saddle, along with several pieces of bridle. So he patched up the bridle, put his papers and chart in a bag, and went out to preach. As far as money was concerned, he depended upon the kindness of those he met to provide food and lodging. Before long he had expanded his sermon bank to six.

Along the way he met a teacher friend who was having a problem with his eyes. The friend asked James to substitute-teach for him for a week. It was a medical emergency, and James readily agreed, for it was a good opportunity. He'd teach in the schoolhouse at Burnham during the day, and hold meetings there in the evenings. This would give him a week of meetings—it was a good thing he now had six sermons! He could easily expand them into seven.

The meetings at Burnham were a great success, and 60 people committed their lives to Christ. James was unprepared for such an outstanding response, and didn't quite know what to do with these 60 new Christians. His brother Samuel had been a minister for five years, so James asked him to come and help. Samuel eagerly responded, and spent about six weeks in Burnham, baptizing the people and organizing a church. The Lord blessed James's first efforts in a mighty way, and he was encouraged.

His next stop was near Augusta, the capital of Maine, where he held meetings in a schoolhouse. He gave a powerful sermon to a capacity audience that first night. There wasn't even standing room inside, and on the outside dozens of people looked and listened through the windows and doors.

Then Satan took matters in hand, and the next night a bunch of ruffians tried to scare White into quitting. One of them threw a railroad spike that hit him in the head. At that point he probably didn't have a plan for further use of the spike, but he picked it up and slipped it into his pocket anyway.

The next evening the house was filled to overflowing. Not only were there sincere seekers for truth, but a mob surrounded the building, just waiting to make trouble for the young preacher.

As James walked toward the front of the room, someone warned him that there might be trouble, so instead of kneeling to pray he stood, praying with his eyes open. He saw the first snowball as it came whistling through the window and splattered on the ceiling. That was only the beginning. The mob screamed and yelled so loud that nobody could hear. James and his Bible were soon wet from countless snowballs, and the noise level was deafening.

Enough was enough!

Closing his Bible, James White stepped away from the pulpit and, in a voice that carried far beyond the edges of the crowd outside, began to describe the terrible scenes of the judgment day. God gave him more than adequate language to describe the judgment scenes, as well as the power of voice to make himself heard. None could misunderstand what the judgment of God would mean for them.

As he talked, the mob quieted. There was something about this man that demanded respect. Suddenly remembering the long spike thrown at him the night before, he took it out of his pocket and held it up for all to see. It had hit him in the forehead, leaving a cut and severe bruising, which people could also see. James assured the people that he held no ill feelings toward the man who had thrown it; he wished God's mercy and pity on him. His next words drove home the point:

"Why should I resent this insult when my Master had spikes such as this driven through His hands?"

The men who had caused such an uproar had become very quiet, listening to every word. Nearly 100 people asked for prayers that night. And pray for them Mr. White did, in voice and language such as they'd never before heard. It was a subdued and changed crowd that listened reverently to the closing prayer.

Dismissing the people, young James was trying to elbow his way through the crowd when he felt someone take his arm and guide him away from the mob. James didn't know the man, yet he seemed familiar. When they were well away from the crowd, James turned to speak to his escort, but the man was no longer there. He never saw that man again nor found out who he was, but he always believed the individual was an angel.

The meetings went on for another three or four nights with no further trouble, and a great revival followed.

Making appointments in other places along the Penobscot River, the young preacher moved on, usually holding meetings two nights at each place. Someone always gave him food and shelter.

At Bowdoinham Ridge he was invited to preach at meetings that already were in progress. The last day he was there he spoke both morning and afternoon. The sun was just going down when one of the other ministers spoke to him. "Don't you think you should spend the night here with us?" he asked. "It's getting dark and much colder."

"I'd really like to," James admitted, "but I have a meeting tonight at Lisbon Plains. I'll have to hurry to get there in time."

James had been preaching enthusiastically, and he'd worked up quite a furnace of body heat and perspiration. As he rode into the gathering darkness, his damp clothing began to freeze. It was 16 miles to Lisbon Plains, but it seemed a lot farther. Lamps in the farmhouse windows glowed invitingly as the almost-frozen man rode swiftly past. He could have stopped at one of them and gotten warm, and the farmers probably would've fed him too. But he'd made a commitment, and even though he was going to be late, he wouldn't disappoint the waiting congregation if he could avoid it. His faithful horse gave his all as he streaked down the country road, sweat pouring from his overheated body.

Reining up at the door of the meeting place, James jumped down, handed the reins to a man standing by the door, and hastily asked him to take care of his horse. He walked in the door just in time to hear the pastor say, "I'm sorry to have to tell you that the speaker we expected to hear this evening hasn't come. Please rise for the benediction."

"Hold everything! I'm here," James cried out before they could get to their feet.

The minister and people were happy to see him, even though they'd been waiting for an hour. James apologized for his late arrival and immediately launched into his sermon. He was very cold, and his teeth were chattering so hard that for a few minutes it was hard to understand him. But he soon warmed up and was able to preach a sermon worth waiting for.

Afterward he found that the man hadn't taken care of his horse at all. The poor animal stood tied to a fence post without even a blanket thrown over his back, shivering and trembling in the cold, sharp wind. James was angry that anyone could treat an animal with such unfeeling indifference, and hurried to get it sheltered and fed. The next morning the trusty horse was very sick, and he never fully recovered from the effects of that biting cold and exposure. James learned a valuable lesson: Always give specific directions to the person being asked to take care of your horse.

It took James four months to make the circuit on his first speaking itinerary. It was reported that during the winter of 1842-1843 more than 1,000 people responded to the preaching of James White. When he returned home, he was ordained as a minister in the Christian Connection Church, where he held membership at that time. He was often invited to speak on Sunday at churches in the immediate area, and several baptisms resulted from these meetings.

During the summer months he took the opportunity to visit Portland in an attempt to learn all he could from the Advent leaders there. Making new friends among the believers, he was welcomed into their hearts and homes. They had already heard of his successful winter preaching tour. It was on this visit to Portland that he heard the testimony of a 16-year-old girl named Ellen Harmon. He thought her words showed a deep experience with the Lord.

Back at home in Palmyra, James took a job mowing hay with a hand scythe. Hired by the same farmer was a group of rough young men who recognized James as the newest preacher in the area. Resenting his very presence, they put their heads together and came up with a plan. They decided to make things so difficult for him that he'd quit; they'd put him at the head of the mowing line, then crowd in behind him and run him out of the field.

James took the position and began cutting a wide swath. The others took more narrow ones. They soon found themselves getting farther and farther behind. James White knew exactly what these guys were up to, and with every swing of the scythe he sent up a prayer that God would give him the physical strength to beat these rowdies at their own game. And he did, for with each swath they fell farther and farther behind. The second time across the field, James sat down under a tree to rest.

One by one the other men dropped exhausted to the ground under the tree. Then standing before James, hands on hips, the leader of the group demanded, "What're you tryin' to do, White—kill yourself *and* us? We thought you were a preacher and couldn't handle a scythe. But we hafta give you credit for bein' so far ahead of us, and you're the best mower we ever saw. The sun's hot, and yet you haven't drunk any beer or liquor. We give up."

The next summer James received an invitation to go to West Gardiner, a little village about 20 miles from Palmyra. Several children in the village had heard him preach the winter before, and now they wanted him to baptize them. Arriving in West Gardiner, James visited with the parents of the children and found that many of them, as well as some others, were opposed to baptizing the children. A Baptist minister sarcastically inquired, "What kind of experience does Mr. White suppose those babies have had?"

Asking the parents and children to meet him inside the church, he asked the children—there were 10 or 12 of them—to sit on the front rows, and the parents to sit farther back. He gave a short sermon, and then the children each stood and told him why they loved Jesus and wanted to be baptized. They gave simple, clear answers to the questions he asked them.

Turning to the audience, he asked, "Is there anyone present who is now opposed to my baptizing these children? If so, please stand."

No one stood or made any comment, and James led the procession to a nearby lake, where he immersed each of the candidates in the cool water. Because of his love for children, he always felt this was one of the most beautiful and meaningful baptismal services he ever held.

A camp meeting was to be held in Exeter, New Hampshire, and James felt he needed to be there. Inspired anew by the preaching of the Advent message, he renewed his efforts among the small communities of Maine, visiting two—occasionally even three—towns in one day, giving the final warning message, "Behold, He cometh! Get ready. Prepare to meet thy God!"

But Jesus didn't appear on October 22. Along with most of the other disappointed Adventists, James White had to bear his share of scoffing from unbelievers. The day after the Disappointment, one of them met James on the street. Laughing, he pointed his finger at James and said, "I see you didn't go up yesterday, did you!"

James' quick rejoinder wiped the sneer from the grinning face. "And if I had gone up, where would *you* have gone?"

JAMES WHITE MEETS ELLEN HARMON

James White and others still believed and preached that the time left here on earth was short. As he traveled, he met many people who shared the same interests that he did. Two of the people he met were Joseph Bates, a former sea captain, and Ellen Harmon, a young woman whom God had selected to be His modern-day messenger. These two people were as interested in the prophecies and in spreading the good news as James himself was.

It was at one of the first Sabbath conferences after the Disappointment that James White and Joseph Bates met. They were to become well acquainted as the Advent believers met together to unravel the mystery of what had happened that day, and why.

Sometime during the winter of 1844-1845, William Jordan returned a borrowed horse to James White in Orrington, Maine. Arriving in Orrington, where he retrieved his horse, James learned that Jordan had brought his sister, Sarah, and her friend, Ellen Harmon, with him. Jordan had made arrangements for a meeting later that day, where Ellen would relate her visions. Listening to Miss Harmon that evening as she spoke to the group of believers, James became convinced that she truly was God's chosen messenger.

Talking afterward, they found that they had a common interest in the Advent message. She told him that God had shown her in vision that it would be necessary for her to go into areas where fanaticism had made its ugly inroads. She was young—17 years old—and inexperienced, and there would be difficult times, but He assured her of His protection, even to the point of sending her another angel if necessary. She would be able to give God's messages of comfort and encouragement to many of those who were deceived by Satan. With courage and firm faith, she was willing to go wherever God directed.

James was impressed with this godly young woman. As he looked at her, he couldn't help noticing her big gray eyes that sparkled with enthusiasm as she spoke of the love of Jesus, and how concerned they became when she had messages of reproof and counsel to deliver. Neither could he help noticing how easily and frequently she smiled. He rather liked it when that smile was directed toward him. Perhaps best of all was the wonderful contralto tone of her voice—coming from a musical family as he did, he could tell that not only was her speaking voice well modulated, but it was a good singing voice as well. From his height of six feet, her five-foot-two frame seemed almost diminutive, with the top of her head barely reaching his shoulder.

This was only the second time he had met Ellen, and both times her brown hair was pulled back from her thin face and braided into a bun at the back of her head. The blue dress she wore was of good quality and fit nicely. Her mother was excellent at sewing and taught all her daughters that very fine and necessary art.

To say that James was smitten at this point would be a stretch of the imagination, but he definitely was impressed. But more than that, he began to wonder—she was such a small, frail-looking girl; how would she fare if she had to face some of the mobs he'd faced? He felt she needed a protector, and his brain began to analyze just what he could do to ease her situation.

Let's see, he thought, *it's wintertime, and I can't do a lot on the farm, so why not travel with her and the Jordans? I could organize the meetings and help William see that the two girls are safe. I'm a fair preacher, and I could help carry some of that load in longer meetings.*

Ellen and the Jordans were happy to accept his offer to accompany them, and notices were sent out for meetings at specific places. The Lord showed her exactly where help was needed, and gave her definite messages for each place. Some simply needed to be encouraged that God was still leading in His work; others needed to have certain sins called to their attention; still others were headed into fanatical behavior. Several months were spent in traveling from one group of believers to another, as Ellen communicated God's instruction to His people.

The audiences listened with rapt attention as she related how the power of God had come upon her in her first vision, and she was surrounded by light, rising higher and higher from the earth. She told how she looked for the Advent people but couldn't find them. Then a voice said to her, "Look again, and look a little higher." She saw a straight, narrow path on which the Advent people were traveling toward the City of God. A bright light shone behind them, lighting the way so they didn't stumble and fall off the path. As long as they kept their eyes fixed on Jesus, who was leading them toward the city, they were safe.

She saw down through the ages to the second coming of Jesus in all His glory. She saw the triumphal entry into the City of God. There was the tree of life, the river of life, and God's throne. It was a long vision, with much bright and wonderful description. Little wonder that the people were encouraged and their faith revived.

But the Disappointment had confused many, and they were unwilling to accept any explanations of why they had been disappointed. They denied that the Lord had been leading them. There were others who were glad to hear the reason for the bitter disappointment. They were glad for the knowledge that the *time* was right; that it was the *event* about which they had been mistaken. The sanctuary to be cleansed was not the earth but the sanctuary in heaven. And Jesus *would* come to take His people to their heavenly home.

When Ellen returned home to Portland, she knew she'd been faithful in following God's leading. Among other places, she had visited Garland and Exeter, Maine, where she met and counseled some who had been led into fanaticism. It was very hard for her to deal with such distressing issues, but God sustained and blessed her.

On another trip Ellen traveled with Louisa Foss, sister of her brother-in-law, and Elder and Mrs. Files, old friends of the Harmon family. Ralph Haskins and James White also accompanied them. After about three months traveling in eastern Maine, Ellen was back in Orrington, where she had begun her work. She found that fanaticism had taken over, and many who had been faithful had been led astray. The fanaticism had become so wild and unrestrained that the town constables had outlawed any meetings by the Adventists.

A few faithful ones still quietly met together, and Ellen found them to be "especially solemn." She met with them only one time, and the little group was "greatly refreshed." As they were praying together, she was shown in vision that she must return home the next morning.

She had done her part in obeying God, and He had shielded her and those with her from the eyes of those who so violently opposed her messages. But the fanatics were closing in, and their intentions toward Ellen and her companions were anything but kind. Her work there was done for the time being, and very early the next morning the little group escaped to Belfast in a boat borrowed by James White and two friends from the faithful group in Orrington. In Belfast they boarded a steamer for Portland. But then James and the other two men had to row 20 miles back upstream to return the boat to Orrington. Trouble stood on the dock as the boat landed. These were men who were angry that someone had dared hold a meeting in their town.

"Where's Miss Harmon?" one of them demanded.

"She's gone to Portland."

"All right, men. Let 'em have it!"

The aggressors made a dive for James and his companions, beating them with a horsewhip and whatever other weapon they could lay their hands on. Then they dragged the bruised and beaten men off to jail, where they spent the night. The next day they were released to go their way, nursing their various cuts and bruises, but fortunately they had no broken bones.

MIRACLE IN TOPSHAM

Ellen continued her travels, always with at least one other woman and a trusted man, or a couple. This was the case when she went to Topsham, Maine, where her dear friend Frances Howland lay stricken with rheumatic fever. Her hands, swollen twice their size, were so large that the joints of her fingers couldn't be seen. Several people had come to pray for Frances, including James White.

Mr. Howland brought them up-to-date on his daughter's condition. As the doctor could do nothing else for her, the little group decided they must pray for Sister Frances' healing. After their prayers someone asked, "Is there a sister here who has the faith to go and take her by the hand, and bid her arise in the name of the Lord?"

Immediately Sister Curtis turned and made her way up the stairs. Going into the darkened bedroom, she spoke softly to Frances, then gently took her crippled hand in hers. "Sister Frances," she said, "in the name of the Lord arise, and be whole."

Instantly Frances' body filled with new strength. She pushed off the covers and rose from the bed, walking about the room and praising God for her healing. Mrs. Howland heard her voice and hurried into the room, clasping her daughter against her heart and kissing her over and over. How wonderful it was to see her dear child looking so strong and healthy. With a happy heart she helped Frances bathe and slip into a new spring dress of pink muslin, printed with dainty white flowers. With her dark hair tied back by a pink ribbon, Frances radiated joy, happiness, and health as she walked down the stairs, where she was met with fervent amens.

Her father welcomed her with loving arms, drawing her into the large parlor where her friends waited. There they had a joyful season of prayer, praising God for His goodness in restoring their sister, and rejoicing at this visible evidence that He was in their midst.

The next morning Frances ate breakfast with the family and their visitors. As James White was conducting their morning worship, they heard the doctor come in and go directly upstairs to check on his patient. Finding her bed empty, he rushed back downstairs and threw open the door to the big kitchen, where they all sat around the table—including Frances. Astonishment, disbelief, and wonder played across his face. He finally managed to stammer, "So—Frances is better!"

Her father answered, "The Lord has healed her."

James White continued the reading of James 5:14: "Is any sick among you? Let him call for the elders of the church; and let them pray over him." The doctor listened, nodded, and quickly went on his way.

A few days later Frances was baptized. Although the weather was cool and the water was cold, she sustained no harmful side effects, and never again suffered from rheumatic fever.

From time to time Ellen returned home for brief rest periods. When another invitation came to relate her visions, she responded. James White almost always was part of the group that traveled with her.

While on one such journey, Ellen received word from her mother that she needed to come home immediately. Rumors were rampant about her traveling about the countryside with a young man. False rumors, of course, but nevertheless damaging to a young woman's reputation, so Ellen followed her mother's advice and went home.

UNITING THEIR EFFORTS

Not long afterward, James went to talk to Ellen about the rumors. He was an ordained minister; she was God's messenger. It was important that they both guard their reputations. They knew that they must not make any rash decisions, nor do anything that would damage their work for the Lord. Marriage, of course, would solve the gossip problem, but until this time neither of them had thought of ever being married. In fact, James had written quite strongly against marriage. Most of the Advent believers felt there was too much work to be done; the world must be warned that Jesus was coming soon. It was no time for even thinking of marriage.

Seeking the Lord's counsel in such a serious matter, James and Ellen agreed to pray together and separately to find God's will for their lives. After several days of earnest prayer and soul-searching, James wrote of the decision they'd made: "It was necessary that she have one or more attendants. Either her sister Sarah or Sister Foss traveled with her. As our thus traveling subjected us to the reproaches of the enemies of the Lord and His truth, duty seemed very clear that we should unite our labors."

Vignette

One evening Elder White was speaking at a camp meeting service when it began to rain. It poured so hard that it was almost impossible for him to be heard, so he suggested they sing while they waited for the storm to pass. It wouldn't last long. So the congregation sang lustily, "We will stand the storm, it will not be long." The rain abruptly halted, and he was able to continue his sermon.

At that same meeting he became so interested in his own sermon that he walked right off the platform! Without missing a word, he clambered back up on the stage and went right on with his sermon. He worked the incident into his sermon so smoothly that most of the people thought he'd planned it that way.

JAMES WHITE

Ellen Gould Harmon

Messenger of the Lord

The warm days and cool nights had turned the leaves brilliant shades of yellow, red, and gold, and the sun shone brightly in a clear blue sky. It was a day just made for tramping through the woods in the beautiful state of Maine—a day the Harmon children had been waiting for. It was perfect for gathering hickory nuts.

Happily hiking through the woods, Ellen Harmon and some of her brothers and sisters picked up the nuts where they had fallen on the ground. But they also looked for the squirrels' hiding places—that was "easy pickings."

But filling their bags with nuts the squirrels had hidden made Ellen a little sad. She came up with a partial solution. When she found a cache of nuts hidden in a squirrel's hole-in-the-tree bank, she took the nuts but left behind kernels of corn she'd brought along for just that purpose. She knew the squirrels had hidden the nuts so they'd have food when snow covered the ground. As she left handfuls of corn, Ellen said to herself and the squirrels who'd been robbed, "I'm sorry, little squirrels, that your nuts are gone, but here's some corn that I hope you'll enjoy in their place."

❖ ❖ ❖

Ellen Gould Harmon and her twin sister Elizabeth were born on November 26, 1827, in Gorham, Maine, about 12 miles west of Portland. The story-and-a-half house where the twins were born stood on Fort Hill, about three miles north of Gorham. Although the house burned in 1971, it has been named as a State of Maine historical site.

Great-great-great-grandfather John Harmon fought in the King Philip's

War of 1675. As a reward for fighting the Indians in "the great swamp fight," he was given a land grant in Maine. He settled in Scarboro in 1726 and helped establish the First Congregational Church. Most of the Harmons stayed with their grandfather's church, but Robert, Ellen's father, became a Methodist.

A few weeks before Ellen and Elizabeth's sixth birthday, the Portland *Advertiser* reported, "We are told by the early risers . . . that the sky yesterday morning [Nov. 13], before sunrise, was full of meteors and luminous traces, shooting athwart the heavens in all directions. The sky, some say, seemed to be on fire—others add that the stars appeared to be falling." November 15, 1833.

It was the famous "falling of the stars." But in the Harmon home little Ellen slept soundly, snug in her bed, missing out on the spectacle of a lifetime.

MAKER AND SELLER OF HATS

Robert Harmon, father of this clan of eight, found that his business as a hatter was becoming a full-time job—also it was more lucrative than farming. The family moved to Portland sometime between 1831 and 1833. Ellen and Elizabeth had great adventures as they explored the docks and wharves with their older brother John or their father. The Fore Street wharves were crowded with various kinds of ships: brigs, barks, huge clippers, schooners, and even some whalers, though New Bedford was better known as the whaling port. Portland was noted for its trade with the West Indies, and Ellen's and Elizabeth's big gray eyes sparkled with delight at the "Spanish sailors with bearded lips" and intricate tattoos on every exposed part of their bodies. Fore Street was busy and fascinating, and it was a favorite place to spend their little bit of leisure time.

Robert Harmon's hatmaking was a real family business, with each of the children doing his or her part. The procedure was difficult and time-consuming, with many separate and painstaking steps before it became a finished product. Ellen learned to shape the crown of the hat, and that became her specialty. Prices of hats ranged from 75 cents to $15, depending on the quality of the fur used in the process. In those days hard labor usually brought 75 cents an hour.

Word soon got around that hats sold for higher prices in the South than they did locally. Hats selling for $90 a dozen in the North sold for $120 a dozen in the South. With a severe depression in America in 1837, hats became a purchase that could be postponed, and Mr. Harmon decided to take his stock of hats to Georgia, where he hoped to find better sales.

The whole family helped get the hats ready for their long trip south. Each hat was carefully wrapped, probably in muslin, and placed in a large leather bag. The next morning the whole family escorted Father and his precious cargo to the stage depot. The stage would take him first to Portsmouth and Boston, then on toward his southern destination.

The Elm House was an inn that served the stagecoach lines as a depot. Portland was the junction for all the stage lines, and sometimes Federal Street was so jammed with the coaches that it was almost impossible to get through. The best part of being at the depot when a stage arrived was to hear the horn signaling the approach. The drivers trained their horses perfectly in the art of arriving at Elm House with a great dash of speed, almost sliding to a stop at the door.

The driver himself was a picture of splendor. No dusty cowboy hat and homespun shirt and trousers for him. No sir! His were store-bought clothes, with a fancy cutaway coat and a marvelous sash of bright, glowing colors. He even wore a high-crowned hat similar to some that Robert Harmon made. He was a sight to behold.

The children were torn between ogling the driver and saying goodbye to their father. But at last his leather bag with its precious cargo was safely stowed on top of the stage, and he climbed inside. As he waved goodbye and threw kisses, his eyes took in his pretty little Ellen. Little did he know how different she would look the next time he saw her.

SCHOOL DAYS

Elizabeth and Ellen attended the Brackett Street School in Portland. The school never seemed to have enough books to go around, and the teacher often called on her best student, Ellen Harmon, to read the lessons to the rest of the class. Sometimes she was even asked to go downstairs and read to the younger children.

Many years later, as she and her husband were traveling on a train, she was reading one of his articles aloud, and together they were correcting it. A woman sitting behind them leaned forward and tapped her on the shoulder. "Aren't you Ellen Harmon?" she asked.

"Why, yes, I am. But how did you know me?"

"I knew you by your voice," the woman answered. "I attended school on Brackett Street in Portland, and you used to come and read our lessons to us. We could understand them better when you read them than when anyone else did."

The two women enjoyed visiting together and reminiscing about bygone days in Portland.

Ellen's third year in the Brackett Street School brought a tragic incident that changed her life forever. School was out for the day, and Ellen, Elizabeth, and another girl were on their way home. As they started across the commons, a bigger girl shouted angrily at them. They had no idea why she was so furious, but they'd been taught never to retaliate or fight back. This girl was trouble, and they needed to get home in a hurry. Tightening their hold on their books, they began to run. Ellen looked behind her to see how far back the girl was, but just as she turned, a rock smashed into her face. She fell to the ground, unconscious.

Someone who witnessed the attack ran to help the little girl, carrying

her into a nearby store. When Ellen regained her senses, blood still streamed from her nose and face. Her clothing was soaked, and a brightred puddle streaked across the floor.

There was no 9-1-1 emergency service, and she had no immediate medical attention. However, a customer offered to take her home in his carriage. But Ellen, even under such circumstances, was thoughtful of others. Not wanting to risk getting blood on the man's nice carriage, she said that she was all right, that she could walk. Neither the man who carried her nor the customer who offered his carriage realized the extent of her injury, and both allowed her to go on her way with her sister and her friend. They hadn't gone far when, overcome by dizziness, Ellen fainted. Her twin sister and their friend carried her the rest of the way home.

Mrs. Harmon immediately sent for the doctor, then removed Ellen's blood-soaked clothing and washed the blood from her daughter's small body. By that time the doctor had arrived. He examined her carefully, but had nothing to offer in the way of treatment, regretfully diagnosing that she wouldn't live more than a few days. Other physicians were called. One suggested that perhaps a silver wire might be put in her nose to hold its shape. But of course medical anaesthesia was still in the future, and the doctors thought the pain and shock of surgery would just hasten her death. So nothing was done to even try to remedy the damage done to her face.

Ellen lay in a coma for three weeks. As she gradually returned to consciousness, she didn't understand why she was so sick. She had no memory of the accident. Why was everything so quiet? Why were the neighbor women tiptoeing around her bed? Why were they whispering to Mother? From the sketchy facts available about the accident, at the very least today's diagnosis would no doubt be a severe concussion, possibly even a skull fracture. Bones in both her nose and face were fractured, with her nose being smashed beyond repair by the primitive surgery available. Looking at a picture of Ellen in her old age, a modern-day reconstructive surgeon was heard to say that it was easy to tell the injury had caused a "saddle nose."

When she was a little stronger and more alert, Ellen heard a neighbor say something to her mother about her face. She asked for a mirror. One look told her that her face would never be the same. But the most crushing blow came when her father, returning from a sales trip to Georgia, hugged and kissed all the other children, then asked, "Where's my little Ellen?" She was deeply hurt that her own father didn't recognize her.

REBUILDING HER LIFE

One day she was an active, healthy, bright, pretty child. But lives and looks can be changed in an instant, and this was Ellen's lot. God had already instilled in this child of His basic characteristics of love and care for others and a strong perseverance for anything she undertook. Even in this terrible calamity, He watched over her. He had plans for her life.

After several months she did get better, and one day ventured out to play with some of the neighbor children. Most of them turned away and refused to play with her, calling her names and staring at her disfigured face. This was her first experience in being discriminated against because she looked different from other children.

When school started again, Ellen made another unhappy discovery. The words on the pages of her books swam before her eyes. She couldn't read. Her hand shook so that she couldn't write, and she kept getting dizzy and fainting. Her teacher was forced to advise her parents to take her out of school until her health improved. Ellen's school days had ended. For all of her short life she'd wanted to be a teacher. Looking back, she said, "It was the hardest struggle of my young life to yield to my feebleness and decide that I must leave my studies and give up the hope of gaining an education."

In spite of everything, Eunice Harmon, Ellen's mother, refused to allow her to grow up in ignorance. She not only taught her the practical things of life, but added a little schoolwork as well. Mrs. Harmon had been a teacher before she married, and she was determined that Ellen would have an education. Deering's Oaks Park was one of Ellen's favorite places, and she often could be found there studying the trees, flowers, and plants. Perhaps this was where she cultivated her love of all growing things. Though staunch, faithful members of the Methodist Church, the entire Harmon family embraced William Miller's message when they heard him preach at the Casco Street church in Portland. That decision—their joy in the soon coming of Christ—cost them their church membership. It was noted in the records that they had done nothing wrong. Their Christian life was not questioned. It was because they had accepted the truth of Christ's soon return, and this was out of harmony with Methodist teachings. Nevertheless, they were happy in their expectation of the soon coming of Jesus.

Ellen was 17 years old when October 22, 1844, brought the Great Disappointment and Jesus didn't come as expected. As the weeks passed, both her twin sister, Elizabeth, and her brother Robert gave up their belief in Jesus' soon coming, although Robert later reclaimed his faith.

"TELL . . . WHAT I HAVE TOLD YOU"

A few weeks after the Disappointment, Ellen was visiting in the home of a young friend, Mrs. Haines. Several other young women joined them for a prayer service. As they knelt to pray, God gave Ellen Harmon a vision, showing the travels of the Advent people to the City of God, and explaining that the light given before October 22 was genuine. There was no explanation of the Disappointment, but great was the assurance that God was leading.

A week later God gave Ellen another vision. During this vision she was called to share with others the messages He gave her. God's angel said to her, "Tell the people what I have told you."

Ellen was a timid young woman, frail and sickly. She must have looked around to see to whom the angel was speaking. Surely he couldn't mean her! But the message came again: "Tell the people what I have told you."

How could she possibly do what God was asking of her? The angel assured her that Jesus would be with her and guide her, and with this assurance she surrendered her fears to God and began her work for Him.

Yes, she was willing do His work. But how? She was young and thought the Advent believers wouldn't accept the revelations from someone her age and in such poor physical health. Knowing there was to be a meeting at her own home that night, she was so frightened of relating her vision to the little group that she literally ran away from home. She asked someone to take her in a sleigh to a friend's house three or four miles away.

The believers in Portland thought that they'd been disappointed on October 22 because they were mistaken in the time, and that Jesus would yet come in the near future. That, too, had been Ellen's belief before the vision in which she was shown that the time was correct, but the event was wrong. Now she just couldn't face telling them something that was in opposition to that viewpoint. They would never believe her.

To her surprise, a man named Joseph Turner was at the friend's home when she arrived. The leader of the group in Portland, he also edited a Millerite paper. He actually supported what God had shown her in vision, but at the time she thought he took the opposite view.

"Will you be there for the meeting in your parents' home tonight?" he asked her.

"No," she said. "Definitely not."

But he told her that he wanted to hear about her vision, and he thought she should be there. At that she fled to an upstairs room, where she spent the day alone.

Throughout the day she felt greatly troubled by a sense of duty and commitment to God. She had promised God that she would deliver His messages, and now she was afraid. A feeling came over her that God had forsaken her. At last she surrendered and promised the Lord that if He'd give her strength to get home, she would deliver His message at the first opportunity.

But by the time she got home the meeting was over, and the people had gone home.

The next meeting held in the Harmon home found Ellen giving her vision in detail. Instead of scorning her, the believers were happy to learn that there was a reason for the Disappointment. They had heard from others about her vision from God, and now to hear it from her own lips gave them great reassurance that God was leading.

Still fearful, she received an encouraging visit from her angel. "Deliver the message faithfully. Endure unto the end, and you shall eat the fruit of the tree of life and drink of the water of life."

She committed her life to the Lord, ready to follow His leading, whatever the cost to herself. She asked God to open the way, and she would follow.

SHARING GOD'S MESSAGE

Ellen's sister Mary and her husband, Samuel Foss, lived in Poland, Maine, about 30 miles north of Portland. One cold January day in 1845, business took Samuel Foss to Portland, and Mary urged him to bring Ellen home with him. Up in Poland they'd heard of her visions, and Mary thought this would be a good opportunity for that community to hear about them from Ellen herself. Ellen saw the invitation as an opening from the Lord, and she agreed to go back to Poland with her brother-in-law.

It was bitterly cold, and Foss was traveling in an open sleigh. To keep from freezing, Ellen sat in the bottom of the sleigh, covered with a buffalo robe. Meanwhile, the Advent believers in Poland had made arrangements to hold a meeting that night in the little chapel on McGuire's Hill.* Ellen agreed to meet the appointment, but when she stood to relate what she'd been shown in her first vision, her voice came out in a whisper. After she spoke for a minute or so, quite suddenly her voice became clear and firm, and she spoke to the people for almost two hours. This was the first time she had shared her experience with anyone other than the few believers in Portland. Later she wrote that "in this meeting the power of the Lord came upon me and on the people.

"When my message was ended, my voice was gone until I stood before the people again, when the same singular restoration was repeated. I felt a constant assurance that I was doing the will of God, and saw marked results attending my efforts."

As her confidence in God's leading increased, Ellen was eager to follow His will. She determined to go wherever He opened the way. William Jordan and his sister Sarah invited her to go with them to Orrington, Maine, 100 miles away. They felt that the believers there would be blessed by her encouraging messages. Since William had other business to care for there, he took advantage of this trip to return a borrowed horse to its owner—James White, a young Adventist minister.

James White had met Ellen Harmon when he visited Portland in 1843. He apparently didn't make much of an impression on her, for she remembered first meeting him when William Jordan returned White's horse to him in Orrington. At that time she was very favorably impressed by his firm confidence in the Advent message.

A few of the Advent believers became involved in strange teachings that grew into wild fanaticism. Ellen knew some of them personally and commented, "They aren't bad, but they *are* deceived and deluded. In the past they knew what was right and good, but now Satan is deceiving them." Many of the Advent believers waited patiently for further understanding and

guidance from God. Others weren't so patient and were swept off their feet by the teaching that there had been a spiritual coming of Christ on October 22, and they were now in the kingdom. Young Ellen had no idea when she went to Orrington that she was about to be engulfed in a scene of demonic fanaticism.

Some of the former believers she met in Orrington claimed that Jesus had actually come to the world *spiritually*, and was now in their hearts. They were already in the kingdom. Then there were those who believed that they could no longer sin, and that whatever they did was directed by Jesus, who was within them. In other words, it was perfectly acceptable to walk down the street naked, to crawl along at home and on the street, to live with those to whom they weren't married, to speak in unintelligible gibberish, and to engage in many other strange and unnatural performances.

Four months later when Ellen again visited Orrington, she found that those she had trusted during her first visit could not be trusted now. Joseph Turner was among them.

As she traveled about, relating her visions and encouraging the believers in various areas, her sister or some other woman always accompanied her. Often Louisa Foss, the sister of Ellen's brother-in-law Samuel Foss, was her traveling companion. Elder and Mrs. Files, old friends of the Harmon family, often went with them. Ellen never traveled alone with James White.

In the late spring of 1845 she was directed to visit the believers in New Hampshire. Joseph Turner learned of her proposed trip and came to her home, volunteering to take her wherever she needed to go. He was driving a beautiful new buggy, and they would travel in style.

"No" was Ellen's answer to Turner's insistent invitation.

"But Ellen," he said, "the Lord has told me that I must be your escort."

"No, He has not" was her firm reply. "I've had my special orders. Elder James White is the one I may trust."

Many years later she spoke of the incident. "This man wanted to get some power over me. But he didn't get it, because I wouldn't ride a rod with him."

The Lord had warned her that there would be men who would come to her with a great burden to take her somewhere, but she wasn't to go with them. James White was one she could trust. He would take care of her, and no harm would come to her.

In New Hampshire Ellen was confronted for the first time with "spiritual magnetism," described as being similar to mesmerism. In Claremont she was told that there were two divisions of Adventists—one side holding to their former faith, the other denying it. She was delighted to learn that at least some were faithful in their beliefs. Elders Bennett and Bellings were two of the "faithful."

Visiting with the two men, she learned that they claimed to be sanctified. They thought they were above the possibility of sin and were completely consecrated to God. They wore expensive clothing and had an air of comfort and assurance.

Then a little boy, about 8 years old, came into the room. His clothes were ragged and dirty. It came as a great surprise to Ellen to learn that this "little specimen of neglect" was the son of Elder Bennett. The mother was embarrassed, but the father was completely unconcerned, and continued talking of his great spiritual attainment. He appeared not even to notice his son. Such "sanctification" suddenly appeared for what it was. Bennett said that true holiness carried the mind above anything earthly. But Ellen observed that "he sat at the table and ate temporal food."

Bennett ruefully explained that his wife allowed worldly things to keep her mind from religious topics. She was, he said, unsanctified. Ellen was not impressed. She later wrote, "Those who followed their teachings were terribly deceived and led into the grossest errors. I was shown that the daily lives of these men were in direct contrast with their profession. Under the garb of sanctification they were practicing the worst sins and deceiving God's people." Soon after this experience Ellen was shown in vision that fanaticism was becoming a real problem in Portland, and that she must return home. When she got there, she found the little band in great confusion and discouragement. During the first meeting held after her return, she was shown in vision that Joseph Turner had fallen into fanaticism.

After she came out of vision, those who were there told her that she had spoken of what she was seeing regarding Mr. Turner. In vision Ellen had reproved him for sin that was not widely known at that time, but that was confirmed by his wife as she talked with Ellen. Turner's work "led to corruption, instead of purity and holiness." He opposed the testimony, of course, saying she was under a wrong influence.

Robert and Eunice Harmon, whose home had been the usual meeting place of the Advent believers, were upset and revolted by the fanaticism now raging in Portland. They closed their home and went to Poland to stay with their two married daughters until common sense once again reigned with the believers.

Because of the testimony she gave revealing Joseph Turner's true spiritual condition, he made it his aim to discredit Ellen, spreading lies that would cripple her influence and justify himself. He even was successful in turning several of her friends and relatives against her. She was so disappointed and discouraged that she became deathly ill.

But the Lord sent faithful Christians to pray with and for her, and Satan's power was broken. She was given a vision in which she was reassured that in addition to her assigned guardian angel, when necessary the Lord would send another to strengthen and encourage her. Then she was shown, for the first time, the glory of the new earth. James White published that vision in the *Present Truth* of November 1850.

"In the spring of 1845 the author of the vision published in this paper was very sick, nigh unto death," the article began. "The elders of the church were called, and the directions of the apostle (James 5:14, 15) were strictly followed. God heard, answered, and healed the sick. The Holy Spirit filled the room, and she had a vision of the 'city,' 'life's pure river,' 'green fields,' 'roses of Sharon,' 'songs of lovely birds,' the 'harps,' 'palms,' 'robes,' 'crowns,' the 'Mount Zion,' the 'tree of life,' and the 'King of that country' mentioned in the hymn. A brother took up his pen, and in a very short time composed the hymn from the visions."

That "brother" was William Hyde, who himself was healed of a deadly illness, and who was present when Ellen Harmon was given this vision of the new earth. Hyde made notes and, as she related the vision, used them as the basis of a hymn. Titled "We Have Heard," it was soon published in several Advent papers, and James White included it in his 1849 *Hymns for God's Peculiar People Who Keep the Commandments of God and the Faith of Jesus.* The familiar words are found in the 1985 *SDA Hymnal*, hymn number 453:

> "We have heard from the bright, the holy land; we have heard, and our hearts are glad;
> For we were a lonely pilgrim band, and weary, worn, and sad.
> They tell us the saints have a dwelling there—no longer are homeless ones;
> And we know that the goodly land is fair, where life's pure river runs."

Ellen was faced with so much criticism and accusation that one morning as the Harmon family met for worship and the Spirit of God began to come upon her, the thought crossed her mind that perhaps this was the mesmerism of which she had been accused. She resisted the Spirit, and immediately was struck dumb. She knew nothing for a few minutes and then was shown her sin in resisting the power of God. For the next 24 hours she was unable to speak. In the vision she saw a card on which 50 texts of Scripture were written in gold.

Coming out of vision, she motioned for a slate; on it she wrote that she couldn't speak. She asked for the large Bible, remembering and quickly turning to all the texts she'd seen in vision. Early the next morning, when her ability to speak was restored, the household awakened to her shouts of praises to God. Never again did she doubt or resist the power of God, no matter what others might think of her.

That trial marked a turning point in her life. Until that time she had been unable to write because her hand trembled so much that she couldn't hold a pen steady. In vision she picked up a pen and found that she could write with a steady hand. From that time on, her nerves were strengthened, and her hand became steady. She could write without weariness. Her right hand almost never tired and rarely trembled.

TROUBLING TESTIMONIES

It was very difficult for Ellen to relate the plain and sometimes sharp reproofs God gave her for certain individuals, and she sometimes tried to soften the messages and cushion the censure. Then she would agonize over whether she'd phrased the message just right, or whether she'd done all she could for the person. She often felt death would have been preferable to ever having another vision of counsel for others.

In answer to her agonizing distress, God sent her a special message in a vision: She saw Jesus look at her with a frown and then turn away from her. Jesus turned away from her! Oh, she couldn't bear it! This must be how the lost will feel when they cry for the mountains to fall upon them. Then the angel spoke to her and lifted her to her feet. She was shown what would happen if she didn't faithfully deliver God's messages.

"A company was presented before me whose hair and garments were torn, and whose countenances were the very picture of despair and horror. They came close to me, and took their garments and rubbed them on mine. I looked at my garments and saw that they were stained with blood."

The angel assured her that this scenario hadn't been played out yet; it was just a warning that if she failed in delivering the counsels God sent, the blood of those who were lost would be upon her. Realizing what a terrible fate that would be, she willingly delivered the messages God sent, regardless of her own feelings. God's grace was sufficient for her.

God sent Ellen to Paris, Maine, where she was instructed to deliver His warning to an Elder Stevens. He seemed to be a faithful and devoted Christian, and some of the people even believed that he was especially directed by God Himself.

Now, Elder Stevens had called a meeting to give some kind of important news that he had "received," and he was somewhat unhappy when he saw Ellen there. But he opened the meeting with prayer, and, as Ellen began to pray, she was taken away in vision. She was shown the teachings of the Bible in contrast with the teachings of this man.

He refused to listen as she related the vision, but the people could see the inconsistencies in his teachings, and they knew he was wrong. God had sent His messenger to free the people from the wrong influence this man was holding over them. Stevens had become so fanatical that he bordered on insanity.

He charged that the visions were of the devil, and continued to follow the evil spirit that led him until Satan was able to take full control of his mind. His family and friends were finally forced to confine him, and a short time later he hung himself with a rope made of his bedsheets. The eyes of the people were opened, and his reign of fanaticism was over.

After returning home to Portland, Ellen was shown that she must go to Portsmouth the next day and give the message of warning about fanaticism and false teachings to the people there. Her sister Sarah and James White were to go with her. None of them had any money to pay the train fare, but Ellen got ready for the trip, trusting that the Lord would open the way. Just as she put on her bonnet she heard the train's first warning whistle—the depot was only two or three short blocks away. She looked out the window and saw an acquaintance coming up the street in his wagon, driving very fast. Halting in a cloud of dust at the Harmons' front gate, he ran into the house, asking excitedly, "Is there someone here who needs money? I was impressed that someone here needed money."

They quickly explained that the Lord had called them to go to Portsmouth, but they had no money for the fare. They were ready to go, trusting God to open the way. The faithful brother handed over enough money to get the three of them to Portsmouth and back.

"Get in my wagon and I'll take you to the depot," he said breathlessly. The three of them piled into the wagon, and it fairly flew down the street to the train station. Ellen and her companions had barely taken their seats when the train chugged forward. Their faith was strengthened, and they felt much encouraged by this direct answer to prayer. Ellen's message in Portsmouth was accepted, and the people were grateful for the warning and encouragement she brought them.

MORE FANATICISM

Two men, Mr. Sargent and Mr. Robbins, were leaders of a group of fanatics in the Boston area. Knowing that Ellen Harmon had been shown their error and deceit, they were decidedly against her visions and severe in their censure and attitude toward anyone who didn't agree with them.

Arrangements had been made for Ellen and her sister Sarah to stay at the home of Otis Nichols, in the vicinity of Boston. As it happened, Sargent and Robbins went to the Nichols home, apparently planning to spend the night. As they stood outside talking with Mr. Nichols, he mentioned that Ellen Harmon was there and invited them to come inside. They immediately remembered that they had pressing business elsewhere. As the two men were leaving, Otis Nichols mentioned that he and his guests planned to visit the group of believers in Boston on the next Sabbath if there was no objection. Robbins and Sargent gave no objection, and it was agreed upon.

However, on Friday night God showed Ellen in vision that there would be no meeting in Boston the next day. Sargent, Robbins, and others planned to leave the Nichols party stranded in Boston while they went in the opposite direction, to Randolph, to warn the believers against Ellen Harmon and her testimonies. In Ellen's vision Otis Nichols and his guests were instructed to go to Randolph, where she would be given a message that would convince the honest and unprejudiced that her messages were of God.

Arriving at the home of Mr. and Mrs. Thayer in Randolph the next morning, Nichols and his guests found a large meeting already in progress. As they entered the home, Sargent and Robbins looked at each other in surprise and gave audible groans. They'd said they would meet Ellen Harmon in Boston. Now here she was in Randolph. The tables had been turned.

After a short break between the services, the meeting resumed at 1:00 with singing and praying. Someone prayed that the Lord would lead in the meeting, and soon after the first prayers Ellen was wrapped in a vision that lasted four hours. During the vision she continued to speak in a clear voice that could be understood by everyone present.

Sargent and Robbins were both irritated and excited to hear her speak in vision. They declared it all to be of the devil. To banish the "power of the devil," they sang very loud, then alternately talked and read loudly from the Bible so that Ellen couldn't be heard. But it was they who became exhausted, with voices so weak from their shouting that they could no longer read.

Ellen's distinct voice was heard by all in the room. Mr. Thayer, owner of the house, wasn't convinced that the vision was from God, but neither was he convinced that it was of the devil. He'd heard that if a Bible were laid on a person having a satanic vision, the vision would immediately stop. Mr. Sargent refused the invitation to lay the Bible on Ellen Harmon, so Mr. Thayer himself picked up the large, heavy family Bible and placed it upon Ellen as she sat against the wall. Immediately she rose to her feet, holding the Bible over her head as high as she could reach, saying, "The inspired testimony of God."

As she looked upward with the Bible balanced on her uplifted hand, she turned its pages with the other hand. Placing her finger on a passage, she'd then quote it. Some in the room climbed on a chair so they could see the pages of the Bible and check the passages as she recited them. They were amazed that she correctly quoted each one.

It was almost sundown, and the candles had been lit, when Ellen came out of vision four hours later.

Otis Nichols gives us the end result of this extraordinary day.

"Satan took control of their minds [the fanatical ones] and led them to confess publicly some of the most shameful acts of their lives, which had the effect to break up the meetings at Randolph and separate the honest souls from their unholy influence. The principal leading ones united with Sargent, Robbins, and a company in Boston called the 'No-work Party,' a shameful company of fanatics numbering some twenty individuals whose principal teachings were denouncing and cursing those who believed in Sister [Harmon's] visions. . . .

"They continued together in this state of feeling some time, a year or more, when they made a wreck of all their faith in the doctrines taught in the Bible and then broke up and scattered, declaring themselves free from all sinning enjoined upon them in the Scriptures."

A few weeks after her four-hour vision, Ellen visited Randolph for the last time. The leaders of the group—Sargent, Robbins, and a few others—still made no confession of their mistakes. She had to tell them that the curse of God would soon rest upon them, and everyone would know it. It came to pass just as she said.

CHALLENGED BY JOSEPH BATES

Ellen and her sister Sarah became acquainted with Captain Joseph Bates as they attended meetings in New Bedford, Massachusetts. Captain Bates had accumulated a fortune during his seafaring days, and he used it in spreading the Advent message and the truth about the Sabbath. He'd heard of Miss Harmon and her visions and was concerned about them. Although he could see nothing in her visions that went against the teachings of Scripture, he just couldn't accept them. "I'm a doubting Thomas," he told her. "I don't believe in visions."

Still, Bates took every opportunity to question her and get to the truth. When she was in vision, he watched carefully to see if he could detect any signs of mesmerism or deception. As a result of his own investigations he came to believe that her work truly was of God, and he accepted her visions as such.

Ellen found Captain Bates to be a true Christian gentleman, kind and courteous. He kept the seventh-day Sabbath, feeling it was of utmost importance. She couldn't quite see it that way, and thought he was mistaken in dwelling so forcefully upon the fourth commandment.

And so it was that God led His children, one step at a time. In spite of the Great Disappointment of October 22, 1844, they fully expected Him to lead them in His ways. He gave Ellen Harmon a vision in which she was shown Christ as He entered the Most Holy Place in the heavenly sanctuary to begin another phase of His ministry. It also affirmed further conclusions as they studied the Bible prophecies in depth.

As for James White's place in Ellen's life, after much prayer and seeking of God's guidance, they felt it was His will that they become life companions.

* More recent information has come to the White Estate from a McGuire descendant that there was no chapel on the hill at that time, and that the meeting was held in the McGuire home.

Vignettes

The "large" Bible Ellen asked for the day she was "struck dumb" was the same "big Bible" that can be seen today in the vault at the Ellen G. White Estate at the General Conference headquarters. At one time it had the names of Robert and Eunice Harmon engraved in gold on the spine. So many believers from around the world have had the privilege of holding the 18.5-pound Bible that the letters have long since been worn away. The Bible is 11 by 18 inches, and four inches thick. Printed in Boston in 1822, it's a Joseph Teal Bible, including the apocrypha, and illustrated with 26 steel engravings. Between the Old and New Testaments is a page bearing the family record in James White's handwriting.

This is the same Bible that Ellen Harmon held in vision for almost a half hour. It was during family worship in her parents' home that the vision occurred during which she picked up the heavy Bible, holding it on her left hand with her arm stretched out full length at shoulder level. This vision stressed the value and importance of studying the Word of God. At the time Ellen weighed only about 80 pounds, and was in such frail health that it would have been impossible for her to hold the Bible in her own strength. It was a time of religious fanaticism in the eastern United States, with many people claiming to have visions. The vision with the large Bible was just one of the ways the Lord used to show the people that He truly was guiding this young woman, and that He had a work for her to do.

The account of this experience has come down through the family from Robert and Eunice Harmon, to James White, to his son, William C. White, who told it to his son, Arthur L. White, who for many years was director of the Ellen G. White Estate.

Even as a child Ellen had that special characteristic of truly caring about others. One day as she and Elizabeth were going through the woods, they came upon a log that wasn't easy to get across. Elizabeth, who was a little on the chubby side, said to her sister, "Help over log." And Ellen helped her over the big log. Later Ellen sometimes said she'd been helping people "over logs" ever since.

ELLEN WHITE

James and Ellen White

They Worked Together

Comfortably settled in her spacious writing room at Elmshaven, Ellen White was ready for the interview she'd promised to give her son, W. C. White, and her secretary, C. C. Crisler. This little session had to do with things in the past history of the White family, incidents that only she knew or had experienced. Willie posed the first question. "Tell us, Mother, how did Father propose to you?"

This is her interesting reply.

"We had been going around the countryside for about a year, responding to invitations to relate my visions. You understand, Willie, that my older sister, or some other woman who could act as chaperone, always traveled with me. James would go with us to drive the sleigh or buggy, depending on the weather, but eventually tongues began to wag, and my mother heard the ugly rumors. She sent word that I should return home immediately."

Shortly thereafter James came to her and made a little speech:

"'Now, Ellen, something has come up, and I have to go away for a while, and you'll have to get around the best way you can. Or else we must be married. But something has got to be done!'

"And so we were married." Then she followed up:

"And I still say he's the best man that ever trod shoe leather."

The Lord had shown her earlier that she would be safe with Elder James White, but to this point neither had thought of marriage, for they believed that with Christ's coming so near, it was wrong to marry. But James wasn't about to let her reputation be besmirched. They talked over the problem and discovered that they'd grown quite fond of each other.

Ellen tells us, "It was not until the matter of marriage was taken to the

Lord by both [of us], and we obtained an experience that placed the matter beyond the reach of doubt, that we took this important step."

It's quite probable that by this time James didn't want to give Ellen into the care of someone else, or let her "get around the best way she could." And as far as she was concerned, she'd come to rely upon him to the extent that she was unwilling to have him "go away for a while."

Early on, after James was convinced that God truly spoke through Ellen Harmon, he felt led to offer his services to the Harmon entourage. He made arrangements for meetings, helped with the driving and the luggage, and simply watched out so that no harm befell Ellen. She never traveled without at least one woman companion, and often there were two or three.

Theirs may not have been a wildly romantic courtship, but they obviously had great respect and affection for each other. Many years later, recalling their marriage, James said, "She has been my crown of rejoicing from that time to this."

James and Ellen were married on August 30, 1846, by a justice of the peace. Neither of them wrote anything about their wedding. James White was an itinerant preacher, having been ordained as a minister in the Christian Connection. In view of their lack of formal church affiliation (the Harmons had been disfellowshipped from the Methodist Church because of their belief in the soon coming of Christ), as well as their extreme poverty, it's quite probable that their only ceremony was the one by the justice of the peace.

The couple was very poor, and lived for a time with Ellen's parents in Gorham, Maine. Their first child, Henry Nichols, was born there on August 26, 1847, almost exactly a year after they were married.

James and Ellen steadfastly depended upon the Lord to guide them in their important work of spreading the news of Jesus' second coming, as well as the message of the seventh-day Sabbath. They began to keep the Sabbath after they read Joseph Bates's little tract on that subject. A few months later God gave Ellen a vision in which she saw the law of God in the ark of the heavenly sanctuary, with a halo of light around the fourth commandment. This vision strengthened the confidence of the Sabbathkeeping Adventists and gave them a better understanding of the importance of the Sabbath.

The first of six "Sabbath conferences" was held at Rocky Hill, Connecticut, at the home of Albert Belden, father of Stephen Belden, who later married Ellen's sister Sarah. The meeting was held in the "large unfinished room" of the Belden home. By Friday afternoon other Sabbathkeeping Adventists had arrived. Also there were a few who had not yet accepted the Sabbath. The room proved adequate to accommodate the 50 people who came for the conference, one of whom was Joseph Bates, who "presented the commandments clearly and convincingly." The God they served provided the money for James and Ellen White to attend all six of the Sabbath conferences, so called because they were organized by "friends of the Sabbath."

Since the Whites didn't have a permanent home, Albert Belden and his wife invited them to live in their large unfurnished room, actually sending them money for transportation to Rocky Hill. This answered their prayers of where they should go and what the Lord would have them do. An extra blessing was provided in the person of Miss Clarissa Bonfoey, who had taken care of baby Henry the summer before while his parents attended the Sabbath conference. Clarissa's parents had recently died, leaving her with enough furniture to set up housekeeping. She suggested that she bring her furniture and come live with the Whites. She would have a home and when Mrs. White needed to travel with her husband, baby Henry would have a nanny. Clarissa was a happy, cheerful Christian, and it turned out to be an admirable arrangement for all concerned.

The fifth of the six Sabbath conferences was held in Topsham, Maine. There the Whites stayed with their friends, the Howlands. Just two months later another conference was called to meet in Dorchester, Massachusetts, and James and Ellen faced a wrenching decision. With winter coming, travel was difficult, and the Howlands urged them to leave baby Henry in their care.

With much prayer and tears the parents came to the conclusion that it was best to accept the suggestion of the Howland family and leave their 15-month-old Henry with them. When the Whites sadly left him that winter day, they had no idea that he'd live with the Howlands until he was 6 years old.

Mr. and Mrs. Howland and their daughter Frances loved Henry as their own. They gave him the same love and upbringing that his parents would have, and he grew to be a normal, active, well-behaved child. Ellen must have had some of the same feelings as did Hannah, mother of Samuel, as she left her only child in the care of someone else, seeing him only a few times a year. Her heart grieved as she left her little son just learning to talk and experience all the ordinary things of life. But the Lord had shown her that not even her child could stand in the way of her duty as His messenger.

A LITTLE PAPER

Through a vision God showed Ellen that James must begin to publish a little paper. It would be a success from the start, she was shown, and soon that small paper would grow to be like streams of light going clear around the world.

But James had never done anything even remotely like this, and he didn't know how to go about it. Furthermore, he had no money. They hardly had enough to keep food on the table in their borrowed lodgings. It was a hard thing for James to step out in faith and begin to write that little paper.

However, that's just what he did. He called the paper *Present Truth*. He found a printer in Middletown, Connecticut, Charles Pelton, who was willing to take a chance on this young, unknown preacher named James White.

Mr. Pelton contracted to print four issues of 1,000 copies each, for a total of $64.50. Furthermore, he generously agreed that Mr. White could pay him as money came in from the people who received the paper. Surely God was guiding in this budding venture.

At this time the Whites were still living in the Belden home in Rocky Hill, eight miles from Middletown. Several times a week James White walked eight miles down the gently rolling Connecticut River valley to check on the progress of the printing, then walked the same eight miles back home. He had no horse or buggy, and "Shank's mule" (walking) was the only way he had to get there.

One day Mr. Pelton gave the good news. "Mr. White, your paper will be ready for delivery day after tomorrow. You can pick up your thousand copies that day."

James made *that* trip to Pelton's Printshop with Albert Belden's horse and buggy, borrowed so he could take delivery of the entire 1,000-copy issue at one time.

Arriving home, it took several heavily laden trips up steep stairs to get all the papers into their room. A thousand copies of stacked papers covered a lot of floor space. How exciting it was to at last have the first edition of the little paper off the press! James, Ellen, and Clarissa knelt around the stacks of papers and asked God to send His blessing with each one and to touch the heart of each reader. They prayed not only that the paper would be a success, but that it would be a great blessing to all who read it.

They also prayed that He would bless the publishing work that had just begun. Kneeling around the first issue of that small paper, they had no conception of what an extraordinary endeavor it would become, and what it would mean to untold millions of believers in the years to come.

That evening the Whites and Clarissa, and perhaps some of the Belden family, spent several hours folding and addressing the papers. Of course, it wasn't possible to address every one of them that first night. But the next morning James took an old carpetbag that someone had given him, filled it with the papers that were ready to be mailed, and walked the familiar eight miles to the Middletown post office. The publishing work had been launched. It was July 1849.

A few days after that, Ellen gave birth to their second child, a son. He was named James Edson—James for his father, and Edson perhaps for Hiram Edson, the farmer-preacher of Port Gibson, New York, who was such a good friend to them.

The paper was welcomed as a friend into the homes of the scattered believers, and as they read, they sent in money to pay for the printing. James White was able to pay Charles Pelton the first installment on *Present Truth*. Thus it was that the worldwide publishing work of the Seventh-day Adventist Church was begun in a humble, upstairs printshop in Middletown, Connecticut. The *Present Truth* eventually became the official church paper—*The Advent Review and Sabbath Herald*. Published continuously for more than 170 years, it has gone through several variations of the original name. Today it's known as the *Adventist Review*.

There were many years of struggle to meet all the expenses of living, not to mention publishing the church paper in several different locations. At first the paper had to be printed by commercial printshops. This wasn't always satisfactory, and the publishing committee decided they must have their own press. In addition to solving other problems, the paper that heralded the Sabbath would no longer be printed on the Sabbath, as sometimes happened.

The committee voted to establish a publishing house in Rochester, New York. For about $600 they were able to buy a Washington hand press and enough paper and other supplies to get started. Announcements in the *Review and Herald* called for contributions toward the purchase price. Hiram Edson had recently sold his farm in Port Byron, and he lent the necessary money to purchase the press.

James White rented a rambling old house at 124 Mount Hope Avenue, in Rochester, for $175 a year. He bought 10 ancient chairs—no two of them alike—for which he paid $1.64, and some antiquated bedsteads for 25 cents each. Their table was a board placed between two empty flour barrels.

The old house was home for all the workers, as well as home for the printing establishment. The publishing was done on the premises, and all the workers lived there. None of them received a salary. They had a place to live—such as it was! And food to eat—such as it was! Potatoes were too expensive, so they ate turnips over which they poured some kind of sauce as a substitute for butter, which also was too expensive to buy. *And* they ate a lot of beans—which brought forth the famous quip from Uriah Smith:

"I like beans, and I don't mind eating them every day. But when it comes to making them a regular item of diet, I *must* protest!"

Only three of the workers were older than 30, but all were there because they wanted to be. They were willing to work without a salary, to share a room, and to eat the cheapest food available—even if it was beans. The work was hard, and there was no such thing as an eight-hour day.

It took three days to print the *Review* on the little Washington hand press. The stitching, trimming, and addressing were all done by hand. John Loughborough punched holes for the sewing and George Amadon stitched them together. In the absence of a paper cutter, Uriah Smith trimmed the edges with his penknife. Years later Smith commented, "We blistered our hands in the operation, and often the tracts in form were not half so true and square as the doctrines they taught."

ELLEN'S SECRET SOCK

One day Elder White came home obviously very troubled about something. When Ellen questioned him, he told her, "It's time to bring out another issue of the *Review*. But we don't have enough paper, and we don't have any money with which to pay for the shipment that has just come."

"How much money do you need?" she asked.

One could sense the discouragement in his reply. "I need $64, Ellen. But it might as well be $10,000."

At that, Ellen opened the pantry door and lifted up a black stocking that some time before she'd hung on a nail on the back of the door. Ellen placed it in her husband's hands.

"What's this?" he asked.

She smiled, but did not reply.

James turned the stocking upside down and half dollars, quarters, dimes, and nickels cascaded onto the table. His mouth fell open in astonishment. Finally he was able to croak hoarsely, "Where in the world did all this come from?"

Ellen's mother had taught her the value of being thrifty and saving. Now she told her surprised husband, "James, you know that I believe a person should save something for a rainy day. For the past several months I've been saving as much as I could. This is a rainy day, and I hope it'll be enough to pay for the paper."

Amazed, James counted the coins. It was enough! He was able to take delivery of the paper order, and the *Advent Review and Sabbath Herald* came out on time!

MOVE TO BATTLE CREEK

For a while it was a toss-up of whether the publishing work would move to Michigan or to Vermont. Since Michigan was farther west, it was decided that that would place the publishing operation more in the center of the future work of the church. So in 1855 it was voted to move the publishing office to the little town of Battle Creek.

A small publishing house was built on the southeast corner of Washington and Main streets in the western edge of Battle Creek. For the first time, the employees had a salary and could afford to rent rooms of their own. There is no doubt that it was a good move for all of them.

A publishing association was formed, and James was at last free from the burden of ownership. As manager of the publishing house, he was to receive a salary—at first, $4 a week; later he got $6. Once the publishing association was on a firm financial basis, he was paid $7 a week.

It was in Battle Creek that James and Ellen White first had a home of their own without furnishing space for the press and room and board for the whole publishing force. It was just James and Ellen, their three boys—Henry, 8, Edson, 6, and Willie, 18 months—and the two women who helped in the home, Clarissa Bonfey and Jennie Fraser.

At first they rented a small cottage for $1.50 a week. Finally they were able to buy two lots on Wood Street and build their own home, where they lived for six years.

WHEN THE SABBATH BEGINS

By that time there was a growing body of Sabbathkeepers, as well as a loosely structured organization. As the general conference of believers convened on Friday evening, November 16, 1855, at 6:00 p.m., the delegates gathered to welcome the Sabbath. The sun had set an hour earlier. The next evening they closed the Sabbath at sunset. During the intervening hours a change, based on the group's study of the Bible, had been made.

Having sailed the seas for many years, Joseph Bates was well versed in the methods of timekeeping in different parts of the world. At the equator, the sun set around 6:00 p.m. year-round. The Scriptures indicated that evening marked the beginning of the new day, and the words "from even unto even, shall ye celebrate your sabbath" (Lev. 23:32) seemed to support this point, regardless of season or location.

Over the years, some had kept the Sabbath from midnight to midnight; some from sunrise to sunrise; some from 6:00 to 6:00. There were a few—very few—who observed the Sabbath from sunset to sunset. Most of the believers stood with the Whites and Joseph Bates—they kept the Sabbath from 6:00 to 6:00. But the church was growing rapidly, and with so many members it was felt that the time had come for uniformity in the time to begin and end the Sabbath.

James White had asked John Andrews to make an in-depth study of the subject and to bring evidence from the Bible to settle the question once and for all. Andrews was not able to attend the session, but he left his paper to be read before the delegates. Using nine texts from the Old Testament and two from the New, Andrews verified that "even" and "evening" of the Sabbath were identical with sunset.

As Andrews' Bible study on this subject was read before the delegates, they readily saw that Scripture pointed to "even" as being sunset, and that the Sabbath was observed from "even unto even." That is, all but two of them could see it. Who were the two? Joseph Bates and Ellen White. She'd kept the Sabbath from 6:00 to 6:00 for 10 years, and the angel of the Lord had said nothing to her about changing. She reasoned that it wasn't necessary to change. For his part, Bates was not ready to accept the findings of young Andrews, and he defended his position.

The study had been voted by a majority of the delegates, but two important individuals had not voted with the majority. It was a point of division and bound to cause problems. This was the way things stood through the rest of the Sabbath and Sunday.

But then God stepped in. Ellen White was given a vision calling attention to several points, one of which was the time to begin the Sabbath. The angel pointed out to her that if light came and was rejected, then it became sin. Before light came, there was no sin, for there was no light to be rejected. She also saw that some thought she had been shown that the Sabbath began at 6:00, when she had only seen that it began at "even." She herself had drawn the conclusion that "even" was at 6:00.

The two dissenters were pleased to accept the word of the Lord on the subject. The matter of what time to begin and end the Sabbath was forever settled by Bible study and confirmed by vision. With this came assurance and unity within the assembly. James White viewed this as God correcting the error at the proper time so that there was no division among them on that particular point.

ELLEN WOULDN'T GIVE UP

During the early years sometimes two general conference meetings were held in one year. That was the case in the early spring of 1856, when another meeting was called in Battle Creek. Members of the Battle Creek church offered to provide housing for those coming to the meeting. The Whites, too, expected a lot of company, and there was a great deal of housecleaning going on, for everything must be in good order.

A couple of days before the conference began, Jennie, Ellen White's helper, was mopping the floors from a washtub of water while little Willie, 20 months old, busily sailed his stick boat in the tub of water. The wood fire burning in the kitchen stove had begun to die down, and Jennie went out to the porch to get more wood. As she passed by Willie, she hailed him with a cheerful "Hi, Willie."

It took Jennie only a moment to pick up a couple sticks of wood, but as she came back to the house she realized that Willie was nowhere to be seen. Then, taking a second look, she saw one little foot sticking out of the tub of water!

"Willie's drowned, Willie's drowned!" she screamed to Sister White.

Ellen White came running, shouting to Jennie, "Was the water hot or cold?"

As Jennie answered that it was cold, Ellen told her to send for the doctor and to get James. Grabbing Willie from Jennie's arms and a pair of scissors from the table, Ellen ran into the front yard, placed the baby on the ground, and cut away his clothes. Then she began rolling him back and forth over the grass. Sudsy water gurgled from his mouth and nose, but he did not revive. She continued to roll him, picking him up every few minutes to look for signs of life.

Jennie ran to the publishing house and got James. He raced over and found their neighbors standing around, watching the young mother working over her child. One of them began sobbing. "Oh, take that dead baby away from her," she cried. "He's dead. Take him away from her."

James firmly admonished the woman to keep quiet. "Leave her alone," he commanded. "She knows what she's doing. No one will take him away from her."

And so the crowd continued to stand helpless, as they watched the young mother feverishly working over the small form.

At last Willie gasped a little breath, and then another. Then he began to cry. Ellen wrapped him in warm blankets, held him, and rocked him, reassuring him that he was all right. Then she put him in his wicker crib, changing the soft flannel blankets one after another until he was warmed through and through.

Little Willie received lots of tender loving care in the hours and days to come. The Lord had blessed Ellen White with wisdom to know exactly what to do. She had asked whether the water was hot or cold, somehow realizing that if it was cold there was a better possibility he could be revived. In recent years it has been determined that a cold-water drowning victim has a better chance of revival than if the water is warm. But this wasn't known in 1856. Even so, it was necessary for Ellen to persist in what was a form of artificial respiration—rolling him back and forth on the ground. But from childhood Ellen had shown an unusual perseverance in anything she undertook. This was a striking illustration of that character trait.

Willie made a complete recovery, and grew up to be a great help to his mother in her work. He had seven children, and most of them had children. They're all grateful for that personality trait of *perseverance* that kept showing up in Ellen's life.

DEACON JOHN

In their later years the parents of both James and Ellen moved to Battle Creek to live with them. An addition was added on one side of the Wood Street house for the White's young sons, and an addition was added on the other side for the Harmons, Ellen's parents. After the Harmons moved from there, Deacon John White and his wife, Betsy, occupied the addition until their house across the street was ready.

Deacon John was a sincere Christian, but had never accepted the Sabbath truth. One day he gave James a happy surprise: From that time onward he and his wife would observe the seventh-day Sabbath together. However, Deacon John had kept Sunday so long that he just couldn't bring himself to work on Sunday. The children often wondered why Grandpa kept two Sabbaths. But one Sunday morning Deacon John got out his shoemaking tools and went to work. Wide-eyed, Willie asked, "Why, Grandpa, don't you know this is Sunday?"

With a twinkle in his eyes, Grandpa answered, "Yes, but I've decided that one Sabbath a week is enough for me."

RAG RUGS

The new house on Wood Street needed much in the way of furnishings. It especially needed carpets. The sitting room below, and the front room above had ingrain carpets. The kitchen floor had two coats of tan paint, decorated by black spots about the size of a child's foot. But the floors in the other rooms had neither paint nor carpet. Here was another place for Ellen White's thrift and economy.

When she wasn't traveling with her husband, Mrs. White spent several hours each morning writing at her desk. After four or five hours of writing, she was brain-weary and felt the need of a change. In the spring and summer she enjoyed working in her large flower garden, but her favorite recreation was braiding and sewing rag rugs. This hobby had a second advantage, providing floor coverings for the carpetless bedrooms.

For years Ellen had cut and sewn her carpet rags into strips, then braided them by hand. Now anxious to get the carpets on the floor of the Battle Creek house before winter, she spent much of her spare time cutting and sewing her carpet rags. She'd sew the rags into long strips, and then instead of having to braid them herself, could get them woven for 25 cents a yard. Her supply of rags was virtually unlimited, as her neighbors gave her sacks and sacks of good material for her carpets.

Mrs. White found this a restful hobby, and the fact that it served a good purpose probably appealed to her strong sense of thrift. It's possible that she'd learned the art of rugmaking from her mother when she was a child. Two or three of her sisters also shared the same interest.

But it was *not* something James enjoyed seeing her do. He couldn't believe that it was as restful as she seemed to think it was. He had tolerated the rugmaking through the years. But now! To think of his wife, whose health was far from robust, setting herself to the task of preparing material for carpets enough to cover the floors of two or three bedrooms was inappropriate to say the least. It didn't set well with him at all.

Furthermore, the prospect of finding her sewing carpet rags when he brought some honored minister home to dinner—unannounced—didn't set well with him either. But when he'd pleaded that she ought to rest, she replied that this was restful to her. Finally, as a last resort, he hit upon a scheme he thought might do the trick. He composed a little song—the only one he ever composed—that he began to sing loudly as he rounded the corner onto Wood Street. This little ditty seems to express his sentiments quite well:

"In expectation sweet, we will watch, and wait and pray, until Christ's
 triumphant car we meet and see an endless day,
There'll be no rag carpets there, there'll be no rag carpets there, in
 heaven above where all is love,
There'll be no rag carpets."

Whether the rag carpet project was finished (which is probable), or whether James's song actually prevailed, the rag carpet sewing was soon replaced with a renewed interest in knitting.

And incidentally, it was these same beloved rag carpets that Ellen took from her floors and sold when James had a stroke and she needed money to move him to the country so he could regain his health.

TERRIBLE PRESENTIMENTS

Three individuals are generally considered founders of the Seventh-day Adventist Church: Joseph Bates, James White, and Ellen G. White. Joseph Bates was the apostle of the Sabbath truth. A near-genius in organizational skills, James White had been a schoolteacher, then a preacher. In her mid-teens Ellen White had been chosen of God as His messenger, and given visions that shaped and guided the emerging church. A name for the church was chosen in 1860. It would be the Seventh-day Adventist Church. Formal church organization came in 1863, with the formation of the General Conference of Seventh-day Adventists.

At a conference in late September 1860, the decision was made to legally organize the publishing work. Proper counsel was sought, and a company was formed in which church members could purchase stock for $10 per share. There was no bank in Battle Creek at the time, and as money was received it was put into the hands of two brokers to hold in anticipation of building a new publishing house in the spring. Quite a lot of money was involved.

More immediate in the White household was the arrival of a new baby. A fourth son completed the family circle. Because the baby didn't have a name for three months, it's been speculated that perhaps they were expecting a girl and hadn't chosen a name for a boy. In any event, they seemed unable to settle on a name.

About three weeks after the baby was born, James left on an extended itinerary in Iowa and Wisconsin. In a letter to him, Ellen wrote, "Our nameless little one grows finely; weighed him last Wednesday. He then weighed 10 pounds and one quarter. He's well."

A couple of weeks later she wrote that the little nameless one was fat and rugged, and very quiet—apparently meaning that he was a good baby and didn't cry much. He now weighed 12½ pounds.

When James wrote, he sent his love to Henry, Edson, Willie, and—the nameless one. In desperation Ellen wrote to her friend Lucinda Hall, begging, "Please—send him a name!"

Out in Wisconsin, as James was praying for his family back at home, he had what he called a "presentiment" that the child was very sick. He seemed to see the baby with his face and head terribly swollen. Worried, he wrote about it to Ellen. Upon receiving the letter, she looked at the fat, healthy baby and remarked that if her husband were there he wouldn't have much faith in his presentiment.

The night after his presentiment about the baby, James had an impressive dream that had nothing to do with the baby. He dreamed that the two brokers who were holding the money for the new Review building were selling shopworn shoes in a disreputable store. In his dream, he thought, *How the mighty have fallen!*

For a few minutes after he awoke he felt some concern that the Lord's money was in the hands of those brokers. But he soon forgot about the dream.

The day after his presentiment, the baby was stricken with erysipelas, an acute disease that causes local swelling, caused by streptococcus. He was very sick, and a telegram was sent asking James to come home as soon as possible. He arrived within two days.

For 24 days and nights the anxious parents watched over their child, using every remedy they knew, and constantly praying for him. Erysipelas is very contagious, and this was a time when germs and viruses were unknown, so probably there was no particular attention given to extra precautions. Strangely, no one else in the home contracted it.

It was during these weeks that the baby was given a name, John Herbert. Sadly, the disease was too virulent, and on December 14, 1860, after much suffering, the baby died. He was the first of the family to be buried in Oak Hill Cemetery in Battle Creek.

Ellen White wrote (not surprisingly), "After we returned from the funeral, my home seemed lonely. I felt reconciled to the will of God, yet despondency and gloom settled upon me."

In the afternoon, after the funeral of little John Herbert, James walked over to the Review office. As he stepped over the threshold, the presentiment and the dream flashed before his mind. Immediately calling his colleagues together, he shared the dream and the presentiment with them. He told them that he believed God had shown them, figuratively, that the money was not safe with the brokers, and they should withdraw it at once and buy stone, brick, and lumber for the new building.

The committee took immediate action, and by July all the funds had been removed from the brokers and invested in building materials. A few days later the two brokers went bankrupt, and the citizens of Battle Creek lost $50,000. The town was abuzz with the scandal, everyone wanting to know how much everyone else had lost. The Publishing Association brethren rejoiced that they could answer the query with a smile and the words "We lost not one dollar!"

In speaking of this incident, James White often said that he felt justified in making the statement that God sent His angel to warn them in time to make certain the money that had been given for God's work was secured in the building materials.

HENRY'S DEATH

During the early days of the Civil War, James and Ellen embarked on a speaking tour in the Northeastern states. They allowed the boys to spend the time with the Howland family in Topsham while they went on to their appointments. Mr. Howland was so happy to have them there that he went out and bought a new piano for the musically talented Henry.

As they traveled, James had another of his presentiments that all was not well with their children. He and Ellen finished up their meetings as quickly as possible and hurried back to Topsham, where they were met at the station by their boys and Mr. Howland.

The boys seemed fine, except that Henry had a very bad cold. However, Henry's cold soon turned to pneumonia. A doctor was called, but after examining the gravely ill boy, he said that there was nothing he could do. As the days passed and Henry grew steadily worse, James and Ellen talked frankly with him about death. He even dictated short notes of assurance and encouragement to his young friends in Battle Creek. He asked his parents to take him home to Battle Creek, should he die, and bury him beside his little brother, John Herbert, so that they might "come up together in the morning of the resurrection." Sadly, his parents assured him this would be done.

The family gathered around his bed as he said his goodbyes to each of them. Making a little motion with his hands, he whispered his last words: "Heaven is sweet." It was December 8, 1863. The Howlands were as grief-stricken as the Whites, for Henry had been as their own son to them. At the request of some of the young people with whom Henry had become friends in Topsham, a funeral service was held at the Baptist church across the street from the Howland home.

Then they took him home to Battle Creek in a "metallic burial casket," where another funeral service was held. Then came the final trip out to Oak Hill Cemetery, where he was buried beside John Herbert. Now he lies surrounded by his entire family, all of them awaiting the call of the Lifegiver. Devastating as it was to lose two sons within three years, James and Ellen clung to God, turning to Him for comfort, and continuing in their work for Him.

NATURAL REMEDIES

Brother and Sister Hillard of Otsego, Michigan, were the hosts of a dozen guests on Friday evening, June 6, 1863. The Whites had come to preach at the church there over the weekend, and they and others gathered at the Hillard home for worship. After someone read a chapter from the Bible, Ellen was asked to pray. As she prayed, she was given a vision on the subject of health reform. She was shown 10 categories of counsel, including "natural remedies." These were the free use of pure air, pure water (both inside and outside the body), sunshine, physical exercise, adequate rest, and fasting for brief periods to give the stomach a rest. She also was shown the harmful effects of poisonous drugs used at that time—strychnine, opium, mercury, calomel, and quinine.

Part of the message included counsel about the hoop skirts that were then in vogue. A dress reform was taking place not only in Adventist circles but among others as well. Various groups were advocating their own styles, but none seemed to fit what Ellen White had been shown in vision as being an acceptable reform dress. She decided she would get up a pattern "on her own hook," which would dispense with hoop skirts and tight waists.

Ellen White wore the reform dress for a while, but it was never widely accepted, even among the Adventist women. As styles began to change and women's dress became more suited to healthful living, the reform dress became less important. She advised that "our sisters [should] dress plainly, as many do, having the dress of good material, durable, modest, appropriate for this age." She also cautioned, ". . . and let not the dress question fill the mind."

REVIVING WASHINGTON

The Washington, New Hampshire, church was the oldest community of Sabbathkeepers in the United States, and it was dying. The members had stopped coming, church services were rare, and it had been many months since a Sabbath school had been held. William Farnsworth—the very first person in that church to take his stand for the Sabbath—no longer attended, and the children of formerly active members stayed away because they doubted their parents' religion. Ellen White had been given some personal testimonies for several people in that waning church. Speaking appointments for the Whites were published in the *Review* for a number of churches, but their main destination was Washington. The Whites, along with J. N. Andrews, came to Washington for the express purpose of reviving the church community. James had a special burden for the young people, but realized that little could be done for them until the older members confessed and repented of their sins. As it was, most of the young people had firsthand knowledge of those sins.

It was near Christmas, and heavy snow lay on the ground. Even though most of the members hadn't been to church in weeks and months, they must have realized their need, for the meetings—held in the morning, afternoon, and evening—were well attended.

Worcester Ball (usually referred to as Wooster) openly opposed the Spirit of Prophecy. As the village blacksmith, Wooster's specialty was making axes. He also had been the church clerk for the Christian Brethren church. When the Sabbathkeepers broke away from the Christian Brethren church, Ball had been so enthusiastic about the Sabbath he crossed his name off the Brethren list with such vigor that it was hardly legible. But somewhere along the way Ball became a self-appointed critic of the Whites. He blatantly stood in the few meetings the church did try to hold and poured out bitter complaints against Elder and Mrs. White. He was largely responsible for the gradual decline of church attendance. Nobody wanted to hear his critical spirit and harsh words.

Now, Ellen White pulled no punches as she stood before the Washington, New Hampshire, church. As she gave "the straight testimony" to Wooster Ball, he was able to see himself as God saw him. Sincerely sorry for his sins against God and his church family, he humbly begged forgiveness of church members and of the Whites, as well. Of course they forgave him, though they'd been wickedly slandered by his cruel tongue.

Ellen spoke to several people in the congregation, giving comfort to some and rebuke to others. Nineteen-year-old Eugene Farnsworth—one of William's 22 children—was in the congregation. Listening to Mrs. White give messages from God to one after another, he became convinced that she knew things other people didn't know. He sort of half-prayed in his heart that she would confront his father. Eugene knew what most of the others didn't—his father was chewing tobacco again. He chewed it on the sly, but Eugene had seen him spit the nasty brown juice into the snow, then quickly bury it with the toe of his boot. If Mrs. White knew this, Eugene reasoned, then he'd know for sure that her work was of God.

About the time he was thinking this half-prayer, Ellen White turned to his father and in front of the congregation reprimanded William Farnsworth for his use of tobacco—a sin he thought no one knew. "I saw that this brother is a slave to tobacco," she began. "But the worst of the matter is that he is acting the part of a hypocrite, trying to deceive his brethren into thinking that he has discarded it, as he promised to do when he united with the church."

William Farnsworth didn't escape the straight testimony, and he took it well. He promised that he had chewed his last plug of tobacco. And so far as is known, it was.

A great revival began that day. Parents made confessions to their children, and children to their parents. The Holy Spirit was present in a marked way.

With reform among the older members, James White could now concentrate on the youth. The Holy Spirit touched their hearts, and many of them committed their hearts and lives to Jesus. Twelve of the 18 who said they wanted to be baptized were unwilling to wait until spring when the ice melted. So they sawed a hole in the thick ice of Millen Pond and were baptized in its frigid waters.

Of the 18 young people converted during that time of revival and renewal, nine became church workers, five of whom were ordained ministers. Eugene Farnsworth was one of them.

The church at Washington, New Hampshire, was once again an active and growing community.

CONFERENCE AT GREEN SPRING

A notice in the *Review* announced that James and Ellen White would be attending a "Conference of the Commandment-keepers of Ohio," at Green Spring in March 1858. The population boasted several hundred inhabitants at the time of the Whites' visit.

Green Spring was nothing if not religious. Adams Township had seven active churches in addition to the little company of Adventist believers. However, the reception of James White's preaching in Green Spring left much to be desired. He indicates that it was a "hard, dark place to preach." One of the small towns they visited was Gilboa, a town with three churches and seven taverns. All three of the churches in Gilboa were "closed against them," refusing to allow "Advent" meetings in their buildings. But James finally was able to make arrangements to hold their meetings in a small schoolroom. Even though the place was uncomfortably crowded, James was gratified to learn that their weekend attendance exceeded that of all three of the local churches combined.

Closing the meetings in Gilboa, they moved on to Lovett's Grove, where they met with a new company of believers in a small schoolhouse. Meetings were held on both Sabbath and Sunday, and a funeral was held on Sunday afternoon. James was asked to preach the funeral sermon. After he finished, Ellen felt impressed to say a few words of comfort to the family and friends of the young man who had died.

She had hardly begun to speak when she was swept away in vision, and for the next two hours the funeral was suspended while she was given specific, practical counsel to meet the immediate problems and needs of this local congregation. There followed a broader message for the church at large, a sort of cosmic sweep of the ages-long war "between Christ and His angels and Satan and his angels."

Ten years earlier Ellen White had been given a partial view of this great controversy. Now she was given a greatly expanded, detailed view of the issues and events. She was told, for the first time, to write it all out, and warned by God that Satan would make strong efforts to interrupt her writing. But she was assured that angels would be by her side, and she must put her trust in God.

The next day James and Ellen took the train to Jackson, Michigan. They would spend the night with their friends, the Palmers. Traveling by train gave them time to plan the writing and publishing of the book, which they called *The Great Controversy Between Christ and His Angels and Satan and His Angels*. Writers were very fond of long titles in those days!

ATTACK OF SATAN

Dan and Abigail Palmer were waiting on the platform as the great iron horse chugged noisily into the station. Later that evening the four of them relaxed in the cozy kitchen of the Palmer home, visiting and making plans for the Lord's work. Suddenly Ellen's voice stopped in midsentence. The other three glanced at her and knew at once that she'd had a stroke.

She later wrote: "My tongue refused to utter what I wished to say, and seemed large and numb. A strange, cold sensation struck my heart, passed over my head and down my right side. For a while I was insensible; but was aroused by the voice of earnest prayer. I tried to use my left arm and limb, but they were perfectly useless. For a short time I did not expect to live. It was the third shock I had received of paralysis, and although within 50 miles of home, I did not expect to see my children again."

James and the Palmers also thought she would die, but as they continued to pray for her, she felt a prickling sensation in her arm and leg. She had a bad night, with a great deal of pain and discomfort, but seemed a little better by morning and insisted that she be taken on home to Battle Creek. When they arrived at the Wood Street home, James carried her up the steep stairs to the front bedroom, where she spent many weeks recuperating.

For several weeks parts of her body were numb. When she tried to walk, she staggered and sometimes fell. It was in this condition that she began to write *The Great Controversy*.

At first she was able to write only one page in a day's time, then rest for three days! But as she persevered—there's that word again—her strength increased. Her mind was clear in spite of the numb feeling in her head. Five months later she completed the manuscript—in printed form a book of 219 pages—and the effects of the stroke were completely gone.

During the next 40 years that little book, written in 1858, would be expanded by its author through two more editions, finally to appear as the five-volume Conflict of the Ages Series, with only the fifth, or final, volume bearing the original, all-inclusive title *The Great Controversy*.

It stretches the imagination to realize that those five books—*Patriarchs and Prophets, Prophets and Kings, The Desire of Ages, The Acts of the Apostles,* and *The Great Controversy*—a total of 3,603 pages—all grew from that first 219-page book subtitled *Spiritual Gifts*, volume 1.

The manuscript was about half finished when Ellen was called to the bedside of Sister Hutchins, who was seriously ill and near death. While praying for her, Ellen was given a vision, during which the angel shared with her some previously unknown information:

Satan was responsible for that sudden attack in Jackson. He didn't want that book written, much less published, and he would be more than happy to end her life to prevent it. But angels of God had come to her rescue and lifted her above Satan's power.

Though at first it took a great deal of effort to write, she did her best to record what God had shown her, and He blessed, strengthened, and healed her.

And, for good measure, He healed Sister Hutchins as well.

Just as Daniel was preserved from the hungry lions, and just as John was removed unhurt from the cauldron by the very men who had cast him in, just so was Ellen White's life preserved from the malicious attack of Satan in 1858. She had a work to do. God wanted a special book to be written, a book that would tell the story—the straight scoop, if you will—of the war between Christ and His angels and Satan and his angels.

It's no wonder that Ellen White appreciated *The Great Controversy* above silver or gold, and that she longed for a greater circulation of that book than for any other of her writings.

ILLNESS HITS JAMES WHITE

James White was felled by his first stroke on August 16, 1866. Treatment in Battle Creek didn't help, and it was thought best for him to go to Dr.

Jackson's "Our Home on the Hillside." The Whites appreciated the treatments given there, but what they didn't appreciate was the recreation provided and insisted upon. To keep their minds off their physical ailments, the patients were strongly encouraged to participate in dancing, card-playing, and theater attendance. James also was forbidden to take part in any physical exercise. He continued to be in pain, nervous, and sleepless. Overall he made some progress, although it was slow.

Ellen finally decided that she needed to take James back to Battle Creek. They stopped in Rochester for a few days to break the journey, staying in the home of Bradley Lamson, who lived three miles out of town. Friends set up a prayer chain to pray especially for James's recovery. The group met in Rochester at the home of J. N. Andrews, then went to the Lamson home in the afternoon to be with James as they prayed.

The next week the Whites returned to Battle Creek. Prayers for his recovery continued. Health reform principles were used to good effect, but it was slow going. Ellen had to give her constant attention to his care. They took a few short trips to surrounding communities, but for many months he didn't write at all and carried no responsibilities in the church or publishing house.

He was feeble and dispirited, but the fact that James wasn't able to return to his work at the office didn't keep the office from coming to him. Publishing house employees, as well as those from the General Conference, continually knocked on the door of the Whites' home to ask James's advice and solutions to their problems. At last Ellen realized that a change in living arrangements would be necessary if he was to get better. She also felt certain that without the overwhelming pressure of church responsibilities he would regain his full health. But for this to happen, they needed to be away from Battle Creek.

Even though it was midwinter, she prepared to leave town. James must get well, and she would do whatever it took to make it possible.

But the brethren in Battle Creek thought that it was a serious mistake, and that she was sacrificing her own life in going through with such a plan. They felt that for the sake of the children—and for the continued work of God—Ellen should think of herself first and not endanger her own life. With tears, even James's father and mother begged her to stay. They told her that she'd done all she could for their son and shouldn't put her own life at risk. The doctors told her that James would never be well; they'd never known of recovery in such a case. But her answer to them all was "God will raise him up."

In the midst of a December snowstorm James, Ellen, and 12-year-old Willie, with Brother Rogers in the driver's seat, headed north. Their destination was Wright, Michigan. Not sparing the horses, Brother Rogers drove the team, Jack and Jim, through the falling snow. They traveled 46 miles, and it was nearing nightfall before they found a place to spend the night. It was only a "rum tavern," but they were glad for shelter. The next day another 38 miles took them to the home of E. H. Root, at Wright.

Two days later James and Ellen attended the little Adventist church, and James preached for 25 minutes. Both of them preached that afternoon and the next morning.

The change in James was astounding. During the six weeks that they stayed with the Root family, his health continued to improve. They traveled to nearby churches on weekends, and both of them spoke several times each trip.

Greenville was their next stop, where they made their home with the family of A. W. Maynard, staying another six weeks. It was there that they made the decision to sell their home in Battle Creek and move to Greenville. Brother Maynard was happy to help them find a piece of land where they could build a house.

At the end of three months, James had recovered enough to return to Battle Creek. Ellen was grateful to be returning her husband in much better health than when they'd fled town on that stormy December day. At the same time, she was very much aware of the critical attitudes of many toward her decision to take James away. She had no way of knowing how those attitudes had enlarged over the months.

Nevertheless, they both expected to be welcomed when they arrived home after such a long absence. But instead of welcoming arms they found cold shoulders, criticism, and unfounded accusations. It was hard to understand how their friends could fail to be happy that James was so much better. It seemed that both people and administrators were angry with Ellen for following her own judgment, under the direction of God, rather than following theirs. It was a year before the misunderstandings and hateful snobbery cleared away.

James and Ellen followed through on their plan to move to Greenville, buying a small place there. They set out fruit trees, blackberries, and strawberries, and made a garden.

In the back of his mind, James still heard the warning of Dr. Jackson that any physical activity would bring on another stroke, probably a fatal one. As a result he avoided physical work as much as possible. But Ellen knew—from light given her of God—that physical activity was important to her husband's recovery. But how was she to accomplish it? Being chair of the ways and means committee, she set about devising plans to encourage him in physical activity.

First she sent Willie to the local hardware store, instructing him to buy three hoes and three rakes. Not two, but three. When he returned home, she gave one hoe to Willie, took one for herself, and handed the other one to James. He objected, but finally took it. He couldn't do much, but at least he went through the motions of hoeing around the plants.

When it was time to cut the hay, their neighbors cut it for them. James planned to ask them to rake and haul it for him also. But during the two or three days it was drying, Ellen paid a visit to the various neighbors. She could see that they were overwhelmed with their own haying, so she asked them to send word to James that they were unable to help get his hay in; that they were just too busy with their own work. These good people were reluctant do as she asked, but when she explained her plan, they agreed.

James was extremely disappointed in his neighbors, but Ellen wasn't at all discouraged. She suggested that they "show the neighbors that they could do the work themselves." If James would drive the wagon, she explained, she and Willie would rake the hay and pitch it onto the wagon. He agreed to this part of the plan, but didn't know how they could make the stack. (They didn't yet have a barn, so the hay had to be mounded into a stack.) Ellen said she'd build the stack if James would pitch up the hay while Willie raked for the next load.

The Lord blessed all of them with the needed strength, and James later wrote, "I worked from six to 12 hours a day, and enjoyed blessed sleep from six to nine hours each night."

From then on he continued to gain in health and strength. The hay was in, the garden was flourishing, and James had proved to himself that exercise wouldn't hurt him.

A few days later, church members from the surrounding area gathered at the lakeshore, and for the first time in four years James White held a baptismal service. Four candidates were buried in, and arose from, the waters of the lake. One of them was his own son Willie. It was a high day for the Adventist families in that region.

It was during the time they lived in Greenville that Ellen White had a washing machine. C. A. White (no relation) demonstrated his combined washer and wringer to Ellen and others while they visited in the home of his father. He later made "a present" of one of the machines to Mrs. White. Her enthusiastic report was "It does the work well, and very fast. A feeble woman who has a son or husband to work this machine can have a large washing done in a few hours, and she do but little more than oversee the work."

Ellen White was a progressive woman for her time, but no doubt she would be wonder-struck with the automatic washers of the twenty-first century.

Merritt Kellogg, half-brother of John Harvey, was interested in retaking his short-term medical course in order to increase his medical background. He suggested that both Edson and Willie White join him. Then James got into the act and encouraged John Harvey to go with them.

John Harvey Kellogg was so taken with the medical field that James and Ellen financed him for a year at the University of Michigan, and then a year at Bellevue Hospital Medical College in New York. Determined to gain all the knowledge possible, he even took private lessons with some of the professors in subjects not covered in the regular courses. He served as one of the doctors at the Health Reform Institute, then, at James White's urging, accepted the position of medical superintendent. Two years earlier James had been relieved to turn over to Dr. Kellogg the editorship of the *Health Reformer*.

PREACHING, TEACHING, AND VACATION

The first Seventh-day Adventist camp meeting was held in Wright, Michigan. James knew that other conference leaders would be watching to see whether they should follow Michigan's example. He thought that if this venture was successful, there would be camp meetings all over the world.

And successful it was. Within weeks several similar meetings were held in Illinois and Iowa. Every year they became more and more popular, with the Whites in demand to attend every one of them. While James was preaching at one camp meeting in the West, word reached him that a man had just been pulled out of the river, apparently dead from drowning. James left the pulpit, ran to the riverbank, and immediately placed the victim in the proper position and gave artificial respiration as skillfully as if he'd been trained by modern-day methods. The man lived, and James went back to the pulpit to finish his sermon.

It was midsummer 1872, and the Whites were headed for California, but along the way they took a number of side trips. Their 17-year-old son Willie and longtime friend Lucinda Hall, a widow, joined them. One of the side trips was a visit to Ellen's oldest sister, Caroline Harmon Clough, in Ottawa, Kansas. The sisters hadn't seen each other in 25 years, and the pleasant visit stretched to two weeks. Caroline was so pleased to have her sister in her home that she saddled up her horse and rode to three communities within an 18-mile radius, inviting her neighbors to come and hear her sister speak to them. The last Sunday James and Ellen were there was a wonderful day. Ellen preached three times in the nearby grove, and Caroline furnished the music. Ellen wrote of her sister:

"She is an understanding, intelligent woman, living, I think, up to the best light she has had. She is a powerful singer. This is as much her talent as speaking is mine. I think I never heard a voice that would thrill the soul like hers." Caroline had four children in Colorado Territory and wanted James and Ellen to visit them too. They decided they could stop in Denver and spend a day or two with one of the daughters, Lou Walling.

At the Walling home they were happily surprised to meet another of Caroline's daughters, Mary Clough, for whom they soon formed a strong attachment. Instead of the couple days James and Ellen expected to spend in Colorado, they stayed two months. And they found the vacation home of their dreams—had they ever thought to dream such dreams!

After a month in Black Hawk with the family, Will Walling, husband of Ellen's niece, Lou, suggested that they might like to take a pack trip to Middle Park and camp at Sulphur Springs. Ellen thought this would be just the thing to help James recover his health.

Reaching the Continental Divide was no picnic with the thin, oxygen-depleted air. Both horses and humans gasped for breath. When it was time for the descent, Ellen decided she would ride in the wagon with Mr. Walling, but it soon became so rough and uncomfortable that she chose to ride in the baggage wagon, clinging for dear life to the big bundle of tents. Willie described the trip down the other side of the mountain like this: "The roads are fearful. They go down so steep you are in danger of slipping over your horse's head, then through little marshes which are numerous near the top of the range, and where you must work sharp to keep your horse above ground, and the rest of the way over loose rocks and boulders, through creeks and over logs, up and down, but mostly down till we reach the park."

An urgent summons to hurry on to California cut short their camping trip. Five days later they were in Oakland, and it was love at first sight. They never wanted to leave again. Although it was late September, roses were blooming, as well as many other flowers they'd never seen before. As for the fruit and vegetables, they surpassed anything they had known. It was James's stated opinion that "nothing but stern duty will ever call us from this country."

With a successful camp meeting behind them, James and Ellen were eager to see something of San Francisco. The members there welcomed them and urged that they move to California and make their headquarters in San Francisco.

They stayed in California for almost a year, leaving only when James had to go back to Battle Creek for the General Conference session beginning March 11, 1873. In the end Ellen went with him. It was a weary five-day train trip from Oakland, California, to Battle Creek, Michigan, and they were glad to be home again.

A number of important business items filled the General Conference agenda, but one of the first actions at the session was a motion to form a denominational school. This topic received much interest and enthusiasm and marked the birth of Battle Creek College.

James and Ellen didn't expect to remain in Battle Creek very long, and since their house was rented, they made arrangements to room at the Health Institute. On the morning of April 22, residents of Battle Creek woke to another 4.5 inches of snow. After spending the morning writing, Ellen walked the short distance to the Ginley home, where she and James had been invited to lunch. Only minutes later she received word that James was at the home of Ira Abbey. He'd been stricken with another stroke. Ellen hurried to the Abbey home, where she found her husband partially paralyzed. He was anointed with oil, and fervent prayer was offered for his recovery.

This stroke seemed to settle his mind that he needed to turn over the burdens of leadership in Battle Creek to someone else. The mountains of Colorado were calling them. But it was too early in the season to go to the mountains, and there were still things in Battle Creek that needed their attention.

After filling camp meeting appointments in Iowa, the Whites went to their hideaway home in Washington, Iowa. After a couple of weeks in Iowa, they took the train for Denver. They were relieved to be back in the mountains again—James and Ellen, Willie, and Lucinda Hall. They settled into a cottage near the Walling family where they planned to spend the summer. Their prayer was that James would be restored to good health.

But more meetings called them back to Battle Creek. Both James and Ellen anguished over whether to risk his having another stroke by going back into the hustle and bustle of Battle Creek. The stalemate ended by Lucinda Hall taking the two Walling children, Addie and May, on to California with her. Will and Lou Walling were in the first stages of breaking up their marriage, and Will insisted that Aunt Ellen and "Uncle White" take the children and care for them. Arranging to join Lucinda and the girls later in California, James and Ellen went to Battle Creek.

By December 28 they were back in California. It didn't take them long to settle into writing, with some preaching thrown in for good measure.

Once again, in 1874, the brethren elected James White president of the General Conference. They had rented their Battle Creek home to E. B. Gaskill, the General Conference treasurer, and he graciously made it available to them. Relieved of his responsibilities in California, James once more turned his attention to the work of the church as a whole—including the publishing house, the work in the West, and the educational work.

His administrative duties were heavy, so it fell to Ellen to meet most of their camp meeting appointments. One of her speaking engagements was at the meetings in Maine, where she was able to visit three of her sisters. Elizabeth, her twin sister, joined her there and even sat on the platform with her. Ellen wrote to James that "her sympathies are with us, yet she takes no open stand."

Elizabeth never did take an "open stand" for Christ. During the last years of her life she suffered intensely from what apparently was rheumatoid arthritis, with her hands and feet being twisted and deformed. Mary, one of the older sisters, wrote to Ellen that Elizabeth read her Bible every day.

The Whites enjoyed living in Battle Creek at the center of the organized work of God, but their hearts were in California. As General Conference president, James, of course, had an office, but the brethren also provided an office for Ellen. They were anxious to have them stay in Battle Creek as long as possible, and did everything to make it an attractive proposition. She wrote to Edson that "they furnished the nice large room in the Review office above the counting room with every convenience—sofa, sofa chairs, editor's chair, bureau, washstand, and your mother a very nice sofa chair."

From that time on, James and Ellen traveled back and forth between the East Coast and the West Coast, establishing the new publishing house, Pacific Press, on the West Coast, and seeing to the affairs of the Review and Herald in the East. With all three members of the General Conference Committee in Battle Creek at the same time, in 1878 they met to discuss several important matters. One of the priorities was the need for a larger church. With the regular membership, plus 400 college students, patients, guests, and sanitarium employees, there were heavy demands on the available space. In addition there was desperate need for a place with adequate space to hold the many General Conference sessions and other meetings constantly being held in Battle Creek.

Plans were made for a building that would accommodate 3,000 people on special occasions. As for financing such a project, they would call upon the church at large. The proposal was made through a series of articles in the *Review and Herald,* suggesting that the money be raised "by monthly contributions from any and all persons, men, women, and children, who shall esteem it a pleasure to contribute to such a house. That the amount of the monthly contributions be ten cents from each contributor. . . . That these, and all others who can do so, pay one dollar or more each, in advance, during the month of July, 1878. . . . That the proposed house of worship, on account of the manner of raising funds for it, be called the Dime Tabernacle."

The plan was a smashing success, with both children and adults eagerly participating. The Dime Tabernacle served the church from its dedication in 1879 until it burned in 1922.

By the end of the 1870s James continued to waver between retirement and active service. The work of God was so important to him, and he felt his contributions so necessary, that he just couldn't bring himself to take the final step to retirement.

LAST ILLNESS

During the last years of his life, James White had five strokes. The first was the most severe, but the others added their own damage. In the 1800s it wasn't understood that strokes not only caused paralysis but often caused other problems as well, and they surely did in James. He had personality changes. He became depressed and moody, and was often sad and dispirited. He often lashed out at his friends, and couldn't stand to be crossed in any way. Small differences of opinion became magnified in his mind, sore points that kept on irritating. These symptoms came and went, but they definitely changed him from the decisive, sharp-minded man he had been. In late July 1881 James and Ellen were invited to speak at an evangelistic meeting in Charlotte, Michigan. It was nice weather, and they drove the 30 miles in their carriage. Many people in the community attended the meetings. James spoke three times, and Ellen, four. James was uncommonly cheerful and praised the Lord for His mercies and blessings.

He and Ellen both enjoyed the journey to and from Charlotte, returning home on Wednesday, July 27.

Sabbath morning found them in their prayer grove, as was their usual practice. James prayed three times, again and again asking God for special guidance and blessing. The Lord answered his prayer, and their hearts were filled with peace. A bit later that morning they were in their regular places in the Tabernacle. James opened the services with singing and prayer. It was the last time he would occupy the pulpit.

On Monday he had a severe chill. He was no better on Tuesday.

When on Tuesday night Ellen also had an attack of chills and fever, Dr. Kellogg thought it best if they both went to the sanitarium, where they could have proper treatment. Ellen seemed better on Friday, but Dr. Kellogg told her that James was in critical condition. She was taken to his room, and the moment she saw him she knew he was dying.

He understood what was being said to him, and could answer questions that required only a yes or no. He wasn't surprised when she told him she thought he was dying. "James, is Jesus precious to you?" she gently asked. His answer was "Yes, oh, yes."

Ellen and others who were present knelt around his bed and prayed. He was at peace and didn't seem to be in pain. "Jesus loves you," Ellen assured him. "The everlasting arms are beneath you."

Uriah Smith and others of the brethren who had come to the bedside prayed for him, then left the room. They didn't go to bed, but spent much of the night praying for their stricken brother and leader. Ellen stayed with him through the night. He died just after 5:00, Sabbath afternoon, August 6. The funeral was planned for the following Sabbath in the Tabernacle, giving time for Willie and Mary White to come from California. In a gesture of respect to this esteemed member of the community, the day of the funeral many store owners closed their doors even though Saturdays were their busiest day. Among the 2,500 people attending the funeral were 100 employees of the Review and Herald Publishing Association, each wearing a black armband.

Uriah Smith delivered the funeral sermon. When he finished, Ellen White unexpectedly rose to her feet. Despite her grief, God gave her strength, and she spoke to the large congregation for several minutes, praising the Lord for His love and mercy. Steadying herself with her hand on James's casket, she spoke in a clear voice. "My dear Savior has been my strength and support in this time of need," she said. "When taken from my sickbed to be with my husband in his dying moments, at first the suddenness of the stroke seemed too heavy to bear, and I cried to God to spare him to me—not to take him away, and leave me to labor alone."

We can imagine her pausing, remembering their life together. "Two weeks ago we stood side by side in this desk; but when I shall stand before you again, he will be missing. He will not be present to help me then. . . .

"Now I take up my lifework alone. . . . When I saw my husband breathe his last, I felt that Jesus was more precious to me then than He ever had been in any previous hour in my life.

"And now he upon whose large affections I have leaned, with whom I have labored—and we have been united in labor for 36 years—is taken away;

but I can lay my hands upon his eyes and say, I commit my treasure to Thee until the morning of the resurrection."

The large funeral procession moved slowly out to Oak Hill Cemetery. It took some time for the 95 carriages and the hundreds of people who walked to make the journey to the gravesite. The fallen leader was laid to rest in the family plot where his two sons and his father and mother were buried. James White was 60 years old when he died.

He had led in the official organization of the church, and had participated in almost every small detail of its development. Now it must go on without him. His dear Ellen—his "crown of rejoicing"—would carry on alone in the strength of the One who had led and guided them both through the past 34 years. Without him, the years stretching ahead would be lonely for Ellen, but her Best Friend, Jesus, would continue to support and guide her to the end of her own life.

THE HOPEFUL **JAMES AND ELLEN WHITE**

ELLEN, WILLIE, JAMES, AND EDSON WHITE

John Nevins Andrews

"The Ablest Man in Our Ranks"

A band of Indians crept silently to the edge of the woods and waited patiently for the man and his sons to come to the cornfield. That cornfield had been hard won from the stony ground around Taunton, Massachusetts, the rocks dug out, foot after foot, and neatly stacked to form a wall marking the field. A little after daylight Ezra Andrews and four of his sons came into their view, muskets in one hand and hoes in the other.

They stacked their guns against the stone wall and began hoeing the long rows of corn. There hadn't been an Indian attack in many months, and Ezra wasn't too worried as they began their work. Perhaps the lack of visible Indian activity accounted for the fact that the men thoughtlessly let the distance widen between themselves and their muskets. But the Indians, painted for battle, were watching carefully. Suddenly with loud screams and war whoops, the warriors rushed from the woods, cutting off the White men's access to the muskets. Not being able to reach their guns, Ezra and his sons ran toward the woods and tried to defend themselves by pulling up small trees and using them as weapons. But five men and a few small tree trunks were no match for Indians on the warpath. The arrows and tomahawks found their marks, and one by one the Andrews men were massacred.

Mrs. Andrews heard the war cry, the screams and shouts. Rushing to the door, she watched in helpless horror as her husband and four of her sons were slain in their cornfield. She had little doubt that the Indians would make a rush on the house and kill the rest of the family. However, as she waited, limp with shock and fear, sounds of the attack faded away, and a deadly quiet settled upon the cornfield and the adjacent woods. Within her sight and hearing not an animal stirred.

A long period of silence persuaded her that the Indians had gone. Her heart pounded wildly as she went out to the field, hoping against hope that at least one of her men was alive. But not one had survived.

Eight members of the Ezra Andrews family had gathered around the table that morning, planning their day as they ate their hearty breakfast of fried potatoes, biscuits and gravy, cornmeal mush, and wild turkey. Now only three remained—Eliza Andrews, her daughter Mary, and her youngest son Henry, who had the good fortune to be sick that day and had not gone into the field with his father and brothers. Numb with shock, Eliza, Mary, and Henry somehow managed to dig graves and bury their dead.

Henry Andrews grew to be a tall, strong young man. He married a beautiful young woman and fathered a large family of sons. Over the years the Andrews clan settled throughout Massachusetts and Maine. During the American Revolution David Andrews, one of Henry's descendants, and his friend John Nevins served together in George Washington's army.

Many years later Edward, a grandson of David Andrews, married Sarah, a granddaughter of John Nevins. They settled in Poland, Maine, where they had a son. They named him John Nevins Andrews, after his great-grandfather. Nine years later William P. Andrews was born into the family. Edward and Sarah had two other children, but both died in infancy.

John Andrews didn't have very good health, and it became necessary for him to drop out of school at an early age. From then on he was self-taught. He always carried a book with him, and whenever he had even a moment he would open its pages and absorb a few words or a sentence into his fertile brain.

He was about 13 when he accepted Jesus as his Savior. Especially fond of the Bible, he taught himself to read it in Greek, Latin, and Hebrew. Before he died he could read the Bible in seven languages.

He lived for a short time with his uncle Charles and aunt Persis in Dixfield, Maine, and went to Mr. Grover's school. Aunt Persis was well impressed with John, though she found him "clumsy and bungling at chores and not very neat." He was six feet tall and wore boots of a larger-than-normal size. She found him a promising student, strictly moral, and with an outstanding reading voice. His aunt pronounced that best of all, he had "first-rate common sense."

Uncle Charles saw promise in his nephew and tried to persuade him to go to college and become a lawyer. He even hoped John might become a congressman, as he was. He offered to pay all his educational expenses, including clothing and upkeep. Since it seemed to mean so much to Uncle Charles, John didn't want to disappoint him, so he told him that he'd think about it. But in reality John wasn't interested. John was in love with Jesus Christ, and he wanted others to know Him too. So in the end he had to tell his uncle that he appreciated the kind offer, but that he had a prior, and higher, commitment.

His decision met with disapproval from the esteemed uncle.

Charles Andrews was reputed to have been quite wealthy and a member of congress. More recent research indicates that he was not very prosperous, and he was a congressman for only a few months before he died of tuberculosis in 1852.

◆ ◆ ◆

The Edward Andrews family attended some lectures during which they heard of the soon return of Jesus. Each night Father Andrews carefully checked all the scriptures given during the latest sermon. As he studied these texts, he found that they agreed with what the minister said. And so he and his family accepted the new teaching and became Millerites. There was a lot of prejudice against those who looked for the soon coming of Jesus, and the Andrews family endured their share of ridicule and sarcasm.

One evening soon after their acceptance of the Millerite message, John was escorting an elderly friend, Mr. Davis, to the meeting. Suddenly a group of rough young men stood directly in front of them, blocking their way, and one of them threatened to beat Mr. Davis with his heavy whip. John stepped in front of his friend and bravely told the gangster, "The Bible tells us that we're to carry each other's burdens. If you're going to whip Mr. Davis, you must whip me, too."

The leader was disconcerted by the courage of the young boy. Trying to hide his whip under his arm, he shamefacedly told them to go ahead, muttering, "It's too bad to whip a mere boy."

DISCOVERING THE SABBATH

After the Great Disappointment of October 22, 1844, the Andrews family took into their home a family by the name of Stowell who'd sold everything they had to help tell others that Jesus was coming soon. While living with the Andrews family, the Stowells' 17-year-old daughter, Marian, came into possession of a tract by T. M. Preble telling about the seventh-day Sabbath. Marian read it and believed it, then shared the tract with her brother Oswald. After looking up the scriptures cited in the pamphlet, both Marian and Oswald were convinced of its truth and to the best of their ability they kept the next Sabbath.

Oswald wondered what John Andrews would think about the pamphlet. He was a great student of the Bible and would know what the Bible truly taught. Marian took the tract to John and asked him to read it. He did, and was shocked. Could this possibly be true? Could they have been keeping holy the wrong day all these years? He began to study the subject, looking up all the texts himself and comparing scripture with scripture. The more he studied, the more convinced he became of the truths set forth in Preble's tract.

In a short time both the Andrews and Stowell families were keeping the seventh-day Sabbath. It wasn't long until seven other families in Paris, Maine, had joined them, including the Cyprian Stevens family. The future wives of J. N. Andrews and Uriah Smith were daughters from that family.

FANATICISM AMONG BELIEVERS

Ellen White had to meet a lot of fanaticism in Paris, Maine, in the mid-1840s. There were some who believed that Christ had come spiritually on October 22, 1844, and that He now lived perfectly in His saints. They also believed that the eternal Sabbath had dawned, and since one does not work on the Sabbath, they refused to work. They "proved" they were spiritually in heaven by "humbling" themselves and becoming as little children. They crawled on their hands and knees. They believed that they were now like the angels and thus were free to take spiritual wives. There seemed to be no end to the fanatical schemes they could invent.

Evidence seems to indicate that the Andrews family was involved in some aspects of the fanaticism, especially the "no work" doctrine. Persis Sibley Andrews wrote in her diary of March 1846: "We called upon brother Edward—who—poor deluded man—with his family still believe in the speedy coming of Christ—that the day of grace has been past this year. They have done no labor for more than two years and have lived in constant expectation that every day the world would be consumed by fire. They have nearly expended all the property of their little community of 'Saints' and nearly exhausted the charity and patience of their friends. Edward said he expected they would be obliged to go to work. Some very likely families, well situated with $3,000 to $4,000 of property, have spent their all, and what is worse have kept their children from school and from industry and educated them only in cant and delusion."

The fanaticism divided the Paris company, and they didn't meet together for several years. But a visit from James and Ellen White in 1849 saw the beginning of better days for the Paris believers. Parents, children, and fellow believers confessed their sins to one another, and a genuine revival swept through their ranks. Ellen White described it as a "green spot in the desert." It was at that meeting that the youthful John Andrews exclaimed, "I would exchange a thousand errors for one truth."

At that same meeting he also made his decision that he must preach the news of the seventh-day Sabbath and that Jesus was coming soon. Not only did he preach, but he wrote many articles for the new church paper, the *Advent Review and Sabbath Herald*.

SELF-SUPPORTING PREACHER

During the next five years J. N. Andrews literally wore himself out traveling from place to place searching for lost souls. He walked thousands of miles in heat and cold, and was so engrossed in preaching the Word that he gave little thought to clothing and food, or where he would sleep. He had only one aim—to reach as many as possible with the gospel of Christ. At first he went by himself through the little hamlets of Maine. Later, in the company of Joseph Bates, pioneer of the Sabbath truth, he went to New Hampshire, Vermont, and Ontario, Canada.

In 1852 Andrews was holding a series of meetings at Rochester, New York. A man by the name of J. N. Loughborough, who preached for the Sundaykeeping Adventists, was encouraged by some of his members to go and hear what the young man had to say and to point out his errors.

Loughborough decided that was a good idea, and he went armed with Bible texts that he felt would prove his points. To his great surprise, the young preacher used every one of his texts to prove his own points. Loughborough went home and restudied the whole matter, then happily joined with the Sabbathkeepers. He and Andrews remained good friends and colleagues for all the years ahead.

Andrews teamed up with Hiram Edson, a farmer-turned-preacher, and they visited the new states in the West. Using Edson's horse and buggy, they covered 600 miles in six weeks. During that time Andrews developed a bad cough and was thin as a rail as he pushed himself to the limit. By day he preached; by night—far into the night—he wrote articles for the *Review*. Edson tried to caution him against working so hard, but Andrews felt like the apostle Paul: "Woe is me if I preach not the gospel. How can I rest when souls are perishing?"

Many were the nights that Edson heard Andrews praying for divine help to meet the many crises ahead. He was especially burdened for O.R.L. Crozier, who had once kept the Sabbath but now was a bitter enemy. Then there was T. M. Preble, whose tract had convinced Andrews and his family of the Sabbath. Preble had given up his faith in the Sabbath and now preached for a Sunday church. At last Andrews felt constrained to write, "I have loved you both for the testimony you once bore to the truth of God. My heart has bled to witness your strange course since. But I leave you to the mercy of God, whose commandments you dare to fight." James White's sentiments toward Andrews were clear: "Thank God for John Andrews. He has become our strongest champion for God's true Sabbath!"

But no one can burn the candle at both ends indefinitely, and John Andrews' candle finally burned into the center. His fragile health broken, it was necessary for him to head home. He got only as far as Rochester, New York, where the publishing work had been set up, and turned in at the gate of 124 Mount Hope Avenue. James White happened to look out the window and saw a haggard, bent man, steadying himself with a cane as he shuffled toward the house. There was something familiar about the man, and James came outside to greet him. The man looked up and, seeing no recognition in White's face, asked, "Don't you know me?" Although the voice was weak, Elder White realized who it was. But there was nothing else about the ill and broken man that he could recognize.

James helped Andrews into the house, where people hurried about to fix him a warm meal. After bathing and getting into one of James's clean nightshirts, he sank gratefully into the warm, comfortable bed. The Whites and the publishing house family tried to nourish him back to health, and James was able to raise enough money to replace his ragged clothes. But he was so ill and exhausted that he stayed with the Whites in Rochester for nearly three months before he was able to continue his journey to Paris and home.

His mother and father were overjoyed to see him, but could hardly reconcile this stooped, thin man with the tall, straight son who'd gone out to preach five years before. In talking things over with his parents, they all agreed on first things first: John needed to regain his health. It was springtime, and perhaps, they thought, along with his mother's good cooking, farm work in the fresh, clean air would restore his health. John could see that his father needed all the help he could get, for his brother, William, was physically unable to do much. As it turned out, hard work, fresh air, lots of nourishing food, and sunshine were just what John needed, and his health rapidly improved. An added bonus was that he and Angeline Stevens were able to renew their friendship.

Then the Andrews family saw an article by James White in an 1852 *Review* suggesting that some of the New England believers might want to consider moving west to Iowa. They could do self-supporting work there while they witnessed to their neighbors. White wrote, "Why not move west, brethren? The soil is rich and deep and easy to work. You will find it very different from the rocky hillsides you have cultivated for years. The harvest field is wide open to you, and the people will listen to our message. The work needed to win one convert in the East will bring in 20 in the West."

And so the Andrews family talked it over. While it wasn't easy to uproot themselves from the land the family had farmed for so long, they decided to sell their farm and move out west. A few months later the Cyprian Stevens family joined them, as well as J. N. Loughborough and his wife, and some of their neighbors. Eventually about 30 believers moved to the small town of Waukon, Iowa. It was here that John Andrews and Angeline Stevens were married on October 29, 1856.

However, the Adventist settlers were failing in their original aim of sharing their faith with their neighbors. Day-by-day living was so hard that there was no energy left over to interact much with others, and God showed Ellen White in vision that her testimony was needed in Waukon.

RIVER CROSSING

Thus it was that James and Ellen White made their infamous dash across the Mississippi River even as the ice melted. It had been good sleighing weather when their travel plans were made, but by the time they got to the river no one knew whether they could actually make it across. All the information they got was that it couldn't be done. The weather had moderated; rain was falling instead of snow, and water stood 12 inches deep on top of the ice, which was getting mushy. As they came to the crossing place at the edge of the wide river, Josiah Hart, driver of the sleigh, asked, "Is it Iowa, or back to Illinois?"

The answer was sure: "Go forward, trusting in Israel's God."

With every breath a prayer, Hart slowly eased the horses and sleigh onto the ice, and the passage across was safely made. As the sleigh reached the Iowa side of the river, the small crowd watching from the riverbank cheered, and the three in the sleigh praised God for His guidance and mercy. Several of the onlookers told them they wouldn't have attempted that crossing for any amount of money. They knew that the ice had broken under several teams, with the drivers barely escaping with their lives. James and Ellen received a questionable welcome in Waukon. Letters from back east had caused the believers to lose confidence in the Whites and their service for the Lord. But Ellen knew the Lord had sent her there and had a work for her to do, and arrangements were made to begin meetings that very evening. With the messages that Ellen brought from God and explanations of some of the disputed issues, the attitude of the Waukon residents began to thaw. Then at one meeting Ellen White was given a vision, which greatly affected the company.

Souls were reclaimed by direct intervention of the Holy Spirit. Confessions and apologies were made, and both J. N. Andrews and J. N. Loughborough renewed their commitments to God and His service. The few days the Whites spent in Waukon were well rewarded. Loughborough returned to Michigan with the Whites, and John Andrews stayed on in Waukon for another two years, preaching in the surrounding area.

ANGELINE'S DIARY

During those years John and Angeline had a son, Charles Melville, born on October 5, 1857. A tragedy occurred the next year when Angeline's father, Cyprian Stevens, was bitten by a rattlesnake. He lived an agonizing five days before dying a torturous death.

Angeline Andrews' diary gives some insight into the family. She tells of Charles being "a rugged little fellow, much interested in his letters." She missed John terribly when he was out preaching, but always wanted him to do what he felt was right and good. She once walked seven miles, round trip, to the post office, hoping for a letter from John. But there was none. Their baby Mary was born on September 29, 1861.

By 1862 John was thinking of moving his family away from Waukon. He was being urged to settle in New York State, where he was holding tent meetings. So he wrote to Angeline, and they decided it would be best to move to New York. She packed up the children and headed to Battle Creek, where she spent a few days with her sister, Harriet Smith. Then it was on to New York, where they had a happy reunion with husband and father. At least it was happy for Angeline and 5-year-old Charles. But 17-month-old Mary wasn't so happy. She didn't remember her father, and she was afraid not only of him but of everyone. But after a few days Mary became daddy's little girl.

John and Angeline had two other children, both girls. The baby born in 1863 lived only four days. She was the first to be buried in the family plot in Mount Hope Cemetery in Rochester, New York. Carrie Matilda was born on August 9, 1864, and died of dysentery about a month after her first birthday. About the time of little Carrie's death, her father was given a special assignment to visit the Provost Marshall General in Washington, D.C. His particular mission was to secure noncombatant status for Seventh-day Adventists. He spent several weeks calling upon various members of President Lincoln's staff, explaining why Seventh-day Adventists believe that participation in combat is contrary to Christian principles. With his diplomacy and clear, eloquent explanations, his request was granted: Seventh-day Adventists could apply for noncombatant service. This ruling laid the foundation for the National Service Organization, which became a source of good help to those in the military who wished to observe the seventh-day Sabbath.

The third president of the General Conference of Seventh-day Adventists, J. N. Andrews, was elected in 1867 and reelected in 1868. He was kept more than busy with general administrative duties, traveling, speaking at camp meetings and churches, and presiding over annual conference sessions. He was not able to do much writing during those two years, but in 1868 he again became a regular contributor to the pages of the *Review*.

BRING A HUNGRY HEART

The first Seventh-day Adventist camp meeting was held in 1868 in Wright, Michigan. Notices of the event appeared in the church paper, which also told readers what to bring in order to be comfortable and to get the most out of the meetings. Elder Andrews urged them, "Most of all, bring a hungry heart. Come up to this feast, brethren."

The people came by horse and buggy, ox team, train, and stagecoach; some walked part or all of the way. The tents—which were not waterproof—were made of thin sheeting. Of the 22 church tents, only one of them even remotely resembled the tents that came later. That tent had been brought from New York State, and was the only one that didn't leak when a ferocious storm of wind and rain descended upon the encampment.

Several ministers preached at different times, but the main speakers were Elder and Mrs. White and Elder Andrews. Of course, they met many old friends, some of whom they'd baptized during past meetings. There were handshakes, hugs, claps on the back, and the repeated joyful question, "Do you remember me?"

Others happily reminded the speakers that they'd been baptized by White or Andrews at this or that place at such and such a time. During this time apart from their busy, tiring lives the campers *and* the leaders enjoyed a happy and joyous atmosphere where God's love reigned supreme.

For evening lighting, stakes were driven into the ground every few yards and a box of dirt nailed atop each stake. Then torches of pine knots were secured into the dirt. Lit, the pine knots produced not only a cheerful light but a fragrant aroma as well.

Each evening, after the meetings were over and people had retired, a tall, bearded man walked up and down between the rows of tents. Beside each tent the man stopped and asked, "Is everything all right? Do you need anything?" If the people inside said they were comfortably settled, he went on to the next tent. If they needed something—such as matches, water, or anything else he could supply—Elder Andrews got it for them. The president of the General Conference was looking after his flock at the camp meeting at Wright's Grove.

One writer described the Wright camp meeting in glowing terms, and made a statement in closing that Elder Andrews had accompanied the Whites in their speaking appointments, and had "caught the same spirit." James White was more than a little unhappy with such a statement and three weeks later wrote in the *Review:* "A recent writer, speaking of the Wright camp meeting, spoke of Brother Andrews as having labored with Brother and Sister White till he had caught the same spirit. Brother Andrews is a man of God. He is a close Bible student. He talks with God, and shares largely of the Holy Spirit direct from the throne. Brother and Sister White often find relief in counseling with Brother Andrews, and listening to words of wisdom from his lips."

ELLEN DIDN'T HEAR HIM

During one four-month period Andrews traveled from meeting to meeting with the Whites, all three of them speaking regularly. During this time Ellen White did a lot of writing—more than 1,000 pages—and all of it, of course, was done by hand. She'd become so intent in what she was doing that she was hardly aware of anything going on around her, as the next anecdote shows. One day when Andrews was speaking, Ellen White sat at a table directly below the platform from which he preached. All during the sermon she was writing, page after page, as fast as the ink would flow. During the noon hour, as they ate lunch and visited with some of the campers, someone asked her what she thought of Elder Andrews as a preacher.

"Well," she said thoughtfully, "it's been such a long time since I've heard him preach that I really can't say."

This comment was received with smiles and even outright laughs, as they explained the scene of a few minutes earlier. She had been so engrossed in what she was writing that she hadn't heard a word Andrews said, even though she sat only a few feet from him.

It should be noted that J. N. Andrews and Uriah Smith, editor of the *Review and Herald,* were brothers-in-law—John married Angeline Stevens, and Uriah married her sister Harriet. Since both men were intellectually gifted, they formed a firm friendship that lasted until John's death. Uriah met Harriet when he came to Rochester in 1853, and they both worked in the fledgling publishing house. No doubt they were instrumental in keeping John and Angeline close to the church during the time they were in the unsettled atmosphere of Waukon.

John was holding tent meetings in Maine as his father came into the last stages of the dreaded consumption. Mrs. Andrews asked him whether she should send for John to come home to see him one last time.

"There's nothing he can do for me," the father replied. "Tell him that I die in the faith and will meet him when Jesus comes." Edward Andrews died in the blessed hope on April 14, 1865.

Anxious to revise his best-known book, *History of the Sabbath and First Day of the Week*, Andrews planned to do that work in the Boston area. Unknown to him, James White asked 200 people to each contribute $10 in order to provide a library for Elder Andrews, as he had not had proper access to the books he needed when he wrote the first edition. Andrews was embarrassed when he discovered how the money came to him, but was grateful for it. And White, eager to have the second edition out as soon as possible, offered him unlimited help from the Review and Herald office. Uriah Smith, also, was so eager for the revision that in the summer of 1871, he laid aside his editorial responsibilities and went to Boston to help Andrews, spending 13 weeks there. Smith felt the results of their research were well worth the time and expense. On the evening of February 17, 1872, John's beloved Angeline suffered a stroke that left her partially paralyzed, her right arm useless, and her speech impaired. With John, the children, and many others praying for her day by day, she seemed to improve. A few weeks later she felt like going for a little walk. It was a beautiful day, and she longed to be outside.

Tragically, she collapsed as John helped her into her coat. Only 48 years old, she died the next morning, March 19.

Her husband paid tribute to Angeline in the *Review*, writing, "I here bear record to the fact that she has done the utmost in her power to help me to go out to labor in the cause of God, and has never once complained when I have remained long absent. During the entire period of our married life no unkind word ever passed between us, and no vexed feeling ever existed in our hearts."

John continued his work for the Lord, but perhaps because of the suddenness of Angeline's passing and her relatively young age, he couldn't seem to get past his grief. He moved to South Lancaster, Massachusetts, and when he traveled, the children stayed with the Harris family.

It was said that J. N. Andrews could recite the entire Bible from memory. When J. N. Loughborough asked whether this was so, he replied that if the New Testament were obliterated, he could reconstruct it. But he wasn't *quite* so sure he could do the same with the Old Testament.

THE FIRST OVERSEAS MISSIONARIES

At the General Conference session of 1874, J. N. Andrews took a courageous and momentous step. He accepted the appointment of the General Conference to go to Europe and establish a work for Seventh-day Adventists there. As Ellen White was to later remind the brethren in Europe: "We sent you the ablest man we had."

Elder Andrews and his two children, Mary, 12, and Charles, 16, sailed for Europe aboard the *Atlas*. As they stood on the deck, they must have wondered when—or whether—they would ever see home again. The ocean voyage took 12 days. The *Atlas* docked in Liverpool, and J. N. Andrews and his children took a train to London, then on to Paris. They were met in Paris by Adèmar Vuilleumier, who took them to his home in Neuchatel, Switzerland. And there they stayed. The house was so large that the Andrews family was given an apartment of their own. They lived in Neuchatel for two years.

Once they were settled in Switzerland, father, son, and daughter embraced the daunting tasks before them. Charles began learning the printing business from the ground up, as well as studying French and German. His father wrote that Charles was "steady and quiet," and seemed to prefer spending time with him rather than with other young people.

As for Mary, she absorbed the French language like a sponge. She was soon reading the proof pages on her father's new paper, *Les Signes des Temps*—the French *Signs of the Times*. She was able to catch grammatical errors that Brother Aufranc had missed—and French was his own language! John, Charles, and Mary were so dedicated to the task of learning this new language that they created a written agreement that each of them signed. It read, "We hereby covenant together that we will use only the French language in our conversations with one another. We will try in the fear of God to keep this covenant, and ask His help that we may fulfill it faithfully. But it shall be our privilege to use the German language whenever we can speak a word or sentence of it."

In his first report to the General Conference, in 1875, Andrews was able to establish that he had discovered other Sabbathkeepers throughout Europe. He especially was happy to report that from all he'd been able to learn there were thousands of Sabbathkeepers in Russia. And any Sabbathkeeper was J. N. Andrews' friend, no matter what their nationality or where they lived.

He also mentioned that he had twice received money from Russia from subscribers to *Les Signes*. One woman had even written him "an encouraging letter."

It was a glad day for Andrews when he received word that the General Conference had voted to establish a printing office in Europe. Plans were made to raise $10,000 to start a press there. James and Ellen White pledged the first $1,000 "for the mission and the press in Europe."

"STARVING TO DEATH"

Basel, Switzerland, became the headquarters for the Andrews family because the best printer in Switzerland was located there. It was in Basel that the first copy of *Les Signes des Temps* appeared in July 1876. It's been estimated that over a seven-year period J. N. Andrews wrote more than "480 articles, or an average of five or six a month," for *Les Signes des Temps*. Obviously the paper took a great deal of his time. He was the major contributor, as well as translator, for appropriate articles from the *Review* written by leaders in America. He planned also to publish papers in German and Italian.

Andrews did more than launch a publishing work in Europe; he did a great deal of personal work as well. The personal contact was one of his motivations for diligently studying the languages, for he had to speak the language in order to make the contact.

The governments of some European countries made it difficult for Protestant organizations to rent churches or halls to hold meetings, so most often the meetings were held in private homes. Even those meetings were often broken up, so it was almost impossible to hold public evangelistic meetings. Many of Andrews' contacts—and converts—were made by personal correspondence.

Dr. H. P. Ribton, in Italy, was one of Andrews' most faithful correspondents, having received some of his tracts and other publications from Basel. In 1877, Andrews was able to visit the Ribton family in Naples. After studying the Bible with them, he had the privilege of baptizing the doctor, his wife, daughter, and another person "in the sea at Puteoli, the port at which Paul landed when on his journey as a prisoner to Rome." Through the continued efforts of Dr. Ribton, within a year 22 persons accepted the Advent message in Naples.

Three years after their arrival in Switzerland John fell ill with pneumonia. A physician was called to treat him, and when the doctor pulled back his shirt to examine him, he exclaimed, "Why, this man is starving to death!" It was true, for in addition to his heavy workload, Elder Andrews was trying to save all he could in living expenses—including food—in order to further the Lord's work. He and his children lived mostly on white bread from the local bakery, graham pudding, potatoes, and sometimes cabbage. They used little milk or butter, and had practically no fruit. Unfortunately, their diet lacked all the vitamins and minerals necessary for health. John spoke of his housekeeper as "about the poorest cook" he had ever met. In addition, toilet and bathing facilities were extremely poor and unsanitary. It's little wonder that John and Mary, as well as other workers, became ill.

But things were looking up. New workers were coming from America to help John Andrews in the work. He was excited at the prospect and took the opportunity of meeting them in London. As an extra bonus of joy, he'd be able to buy printing supplies while he was there.

At the dock he met Elder and Mrs. William Ings, and Miss Maud Sisley, who'd been sent to help him in manuscript preparation. He also met with Elder William M. Jones, his friend who headed the work of the Seventh Day Baptists in London. Jones invited Andrews to preach the two Sabbaths he was there. The meetings were so successful that Elder J. N. Loughborough was sent to England to follow up on the interests.

In Basel Mrs. Ings took over the cooking and housekeeping. She was appalled at the poverty-stricken way Andrews and his children lived. But she took charge and wrote encouragingly to Ellen White, "We can find everything here necessary to live hygienically, and since we have a stove to bake our bread, we are happy."

When Elder Andrews made preparations to attend the General Conference session in 1878, he decided to take Mary with him, for he was almost certain that she had tuberculosis. As soon as they arrived in Battle Creek, doctors confirmed his worst fears. In spite of Dr. Kellogg's warning that tuberculosis was contagious, John spent every possible minute at Mary's bedside, giving her every care that a loving father could. Mary, only 17 years old, died on November 27. Elder Andrews buried her beside her mother and two baby sisters in Mount Hope Cemetery in Rochester. John was alone in America, and Charles was alone in Europe. They had lost their only other family member, and couldn't even grieve together.

Charles wrote bravely to his father, "Our separation will be but short, and then, if faithful, we shall meet our loved ones. So, Pa, don't feel discouraged. We pray much for you."

Mrs. White wrote to John, "We deeply sympathize with you in your great sorrow, but we sorrow not as those who have no hope. Mary, dear precious child, is at rest. She was the companion of your sorrows and disappointed hopes. Through faith's discerning eye, you may anticipate your Mary, with her mother and other members of your family, answering the call of the Life-giver and coming forth from their prison house, triumphing over death. The Lord loves you, my dear brother. He loves you."

She also counseled Elder Andrews that he should marry again, but he couldn't bring himself to even think of such a step. His grief for Angeline was heavy, and he said that his "affection seems incapable of detaching itself from her and taking up some other, however worthy." Yet he recognized that he and his children would have been better off had they had the "care of some good woman."

Andrews stayed in America for another year after Mary's death. On his return trip to Europe he docked in Glasgow, where he had a pleasant time visiting with friends. On the way to London by train, he was struck by chills and fever—something that had plagued him off and on through the years. From past experience he knew he was in for a prolonged illness. He managed to get to the home of his old friend J. N. Loughborough, who was doing mission work in London. He and his wife took Andrews into their home, nursing him through many weeks of illness and recovery. It was three months before he was able to return to Basel.

He was especially encouraged during his illness in London to learn of a Turkish merchant who had read a copy of *Les Signes des Temps* and was now keeping the Sabbath.

Back in Basel, Andrews never really recovered any measure of health. He was so weak that much of the time he dictated letters and articles, and took care of church business, from his bed. But his mind was as sharp as ever, and he continued to write articles in English, French, German, and Italian.

Each month as the time approached for another issue of the paper to be printed, Elder Andrews would regain just enough strength to finish up his articles and proofreading so the paper could go to press. Then he was exhausted till it was time for the next issue.

Hoping that something new had been discovered in the medical world, he sent for the same doctor who had previously examined him. They talked frankly, with John asking what was really wrong with him, and whether he could ever regain his strength.

"You want the truth, Mr. Andrews?" the doctor asked.

"Yes, Doctor. Whatever you have to say, I'll deal with it."

"Well, I'm sorry to tell you, Mr. Andrews, that you have tuberculosis. It's advanced, and one lung is almost gone. The other is severely affected. I can't offer you any hope of recovery."

Upon learning of Elder Andrews' serious condition, the General Conference Committee voted that a day of prayer and fasting be set aside to pray for his recovery. A notice was placed in the *Review* setting the date for July 24, 1880. After that date he rallied somewhat and felt better than he had for some time. Later in the year, Elder S. N. Haskell was sent to Switzerland to encourage and help Elder Andrews with the work.

Haskell soon saw that larger quarters were needed for the expanding work and the increasing workforce. In counsel with the French workers, it was decided to rent a building that had more than twice the space of the old place. Knowing that Elder Andrews didn't have the strength or the courage to even think of such an undertaking, and without telling him of the move, Haskell rented a horse and buggy, and the two of them spent the day in the country. When they returned, the move had been accomplished, and Andrews was astonished to find that his living arrangements had been vastly improved.

Strange as it seems, Elder Andrews had not been given a regular salary. Knowing nothing of how expenses in Europe compared to those in America, the General Conference Committee had adopted an attitude of "wait and see." In the meantime, various amounts of money were sent to him for the work, and he could take his living expenses from this fund. Unfortunately, the money wasn't sent on a very regular basis, and in any event, Andrews didn't feel comfortable taking money from these funds for his own needs. As a result he and his children lived in poverty.

J. N. Andrews was a man dedicated to spreading the gospel to every kindred, tongue, and people, but he was sadly lacking in some of the practical aspects of life. Ellen White had wisely urged him to remarry, for a woman in their household would have made their lives more comfortable and better organized. Had he taken her advice, things might have been very different, and it's quite probable that both he and Mary would have lived longer. But each person works in his or her own armor, and this was the armor Andrews chose to wear—that of a life of such self-sacrifice that it destroyed his health. Perhaps that was all he could do.

WORKING TILL THE END

By 1883 Andrews was completely bedfast. In his last letter to Ellen White, a month before his death, he wrote, "I have given up the control of everything to Brother Whitney. I try still to read the proof sheets of our French paper, but I have no longer the power to prepare any articles for it. I am a mere skeleton and have not attempted to put on my clothes for many weeks. However, I can say that my feet are on the Rock of Ages and that the Lord holds me by my right hand."

One of his last acts was to sign over his remaining $500 to be used in the Lord's work in Europe.

In the fall of 1883, an important meeting was being held in Basel, with representatives from several European countries attending. During the meetings many of the ministers came to his room to give him their greetings and to pray with him, but on October 21 several of them were asked to come to his room especially to pray for him. While his mother stood by his side, fanning his face, they knelt around his bed to plead once more for their friend. As they rose from their knees the dazzling rays of the setting sun filled the room with a golden light, almost as a benediction. They stood quietly for several moments, each lost in his own contemplations. Heavenly angels seemed very near in the room's golden stillness.

Then Albert Vuilleumier, standing at the foot of the bed, put his glasses on and looked closely at the peaceful countenance of his brother in Christ. "Why, he's dead," he exclaimed.

As his fellow ministers had prayed for him, Elder Andrews breathed his last so gently and peacefully that not one of them had noticed. What a fitting way for this modest, unassuming man to pass to his rest.

Elder Andrews had charged his friend and brother-in-law that no eulogy should appear in the *Review and Herald*. Against his own wishes, Uriah Smith honored that request.

Many educational institutions around the world bear the name of J. N. Andrews. In the United States several elementary and secondary schools bear some form of his name, and in Michigan, Andrews University opens its doors to students from practically every country in the world.

Truly John Nevins Andrews was the ablest man we had, and without a doubt on that long-looked-for day, he will "see his Lord a-coming."

MARY, JOHN, CHARLES, AND ANGELINE ANDREWS

Charles Andrews

Hard Worker for the Lord

"Pray, Charles, Pray!" Charles's lips trembled, fear seized him, and his mind raced for words. His eyes were glued to the figure whose fingers had latched onto his father's throat, choking him. His father, trying desperately to pry the icy death grip from around his neck, gasped again, "Pray!"

There was no question in Charles's mind who this figure was. It was the devil himself.

The teen boy's day had started much like the ones that had preceded it. His father, John Andrews, had been working on a book, *The History of the Sabbath*. This momentous volume was a labor of love to share the good news of the Sabbath. John Andrews spent many long hours researching, writing, and editing his work. He wanted to honor the Lord and this important message.

It wasn't unusual for Charles to be near his father as he worked. He would occupy himself with his studies or reading. He knew that what his father was doing helped others learn more about Jesus and His love. The importance of it played out right before his eyes, making an impression on his mind for the rest of his life.

"Dear Jesus, please help my father. Please make the devil stop and leave." At these words the devil dropped his hands and left immediately. "Thank you, Charles." His father coughed out the words and choked as he rubbed his throat. Still a bit shaken, Charles ran to him, checking to see if he was OK.

"He was just trying to stop my writing and preaching, but the Lord is more powerful. He is protecting us." John Andrews' breath was slowly returning to normal, and both had calmed their racing heartbeats.

A short time before, his mother had suffered a stroke and been taken from them. He knew he was not ready to lose his father, too. Often he found himself thanking the Lord for sparing his father's life that day. The incident and the importance of his father's work made an impression on Charles that never left him.

A CRIPPLING START

The power of prayer had been seen before in Charles's life. In 1859, when he was just 2 years old, the family was living in Waukon, Iowa, and his parents noticed that his right leg was not working as well as it should. By the time he was 6, his leg had become thin, and his foot was almost unusable because it easily turned in the opposite direction. John and Angeline Andrews had moved to Rochester, New York, a few years earlier, and they continued to pray and to take him to doctors, but none of the ones he was taken to could offer any solution to his problems.

Then Ellen White received a vision that included advice on healthful living. Angeline wanted to help her son, so she immediately tried the lifestyle changes recommended. To help ease his muscle aches, she used hot and cold treatments. The change offered quick relief to his pain, and his leg began to show signs of strengthening. Next she followed the directions given on the importance of eating a balanced diet, including plenty of fresh fruits and vegetables. A short time after changing his diet, Charles realized that his limp was gone and that his feet behaved like a healthy pair!

These healthful lifestyle changes benefited not only Charles but the whole family. All of them found that they had more energy and fewer stomach issues!

Charles Melville Andrews attended his first camp meeting at age 10, in Wright, Michigan, where he was able to hear such speakers as Ellen White and his uncle, editor Uriah Smith. How exciting for a young boy to be camping and praising the Lord with 1,600 other people! To be out in nature, singing hymns together under the trees. His father, John, was the president of the church at the time, leading the group with an attitude of service. It is easy to imagine Charles joining his father in the evening as John checked with the attendees, walking the rows of tents, checking on their needs.

At 14 Charles would experience the first of several losses of close family members. His mother suffered a small stroke, and he, his father, and his younger sister, Mary, tried to ease her discomfort. As the weeks progressed, it seemed as if Angeline would recover, but then one day, as John helped her put on her coat, she collapsed, and died the next day. Needing a change of scenery, the grieving little family moved to South Lancaster, Massachusetts, where Charles and Mary could attend school and John could continue his Sabbath book research at the libraries in Boston and on the Harvard campus.

THE HOPEFUL CHARLES ANDREWS

FIRST MISSIONARIES

"When will we see our homeland again?" The question came from 16-year-old Charles as his eyes could just barely make out the thin line of land west of them. He could feel the power of the S.S. *Atlas* as it pulled them farther east and into the Atlantic Ocean.

"There is no way to know. It may be many years," his father replied. Mary looked up at her big brother. He returned the squeeze she gave his hand. He understood her feelings of fear and excitement, as they mirrored his own. What an adventure! But also, what an awesome responsibility: to be the first missionary family sent overseas by the newly established Seventh-day Adventist Church.

Charles watched his father's profile. There was no doubt in his mind that his father was one of the greatest, most humble speakers, leaders, and theologians of the time. He had heard his father deliver God's messages about the Sabbath and Christ's second coming; he had seen many confess their need for Christ. *Will it be the same in Europe? We don't even know how to speak the language!*

"Bonjour, mes amis." As if on cue, their traveling companion and translator, Adèmar Vuilleumier, joined them on deck. Adèmar would be returning to Switzerland. He would teach the Andrews family as much French as he could during the journey and serve as a translator until they were able to communicate on their own.

The journey included stops in Liverpool and London, England. They would travel by land to visit Scotland before returning to London. Their last stop would be in Paris, France, before arriving by train at their destination, Neuchâtel, Switzerland. Many of the stops were made so that they could meet and encourage small groups of fellow believers.

Adjusting to life in Switzerland took some time. The three had a tight budget to live on, a different type of food and flour to purchase, and a daily effort made to learn a new language. To learn the language faster, the Andrewses made a pact, which they signed. They would reserve only one hour of the day in which to speak English. It worked! This gave them a favorite hour of the day, but it also sped up their mastering of French and German.

LIFE IN SWITZERLAND

John Andrews knew the importance of having the Adventist message printed . He started right away to put together a paper, *Les Signes des Temps* (*The Signs of the Times*). The printer options were better in Basel, so the family moved the publishing operations there.

Charles and Mary quickly took up key roles in their father's work. They both were able to be of great help to the publishing and production of the paper that John Andrews had started since coming to Switzerland. They had the same attention to detail and quality that their father felt. Mary was an excellent copy editor and proofreader, and Charles took an interest in the skill of setting type and running the printing equipment.

"We will need to cut a new capital S. I see a nick at the top." Charles carefully examined the metal letter, slowly turning the block between his thumb and index finger, angling it in the morning sunlight. Maude Sisley and William Ings peered over his shoulder.

"Good catch, Charles." Maude had print training from her previous work at the Seventh-day Adventist publishing house in Battle Creek, Michigan, later to be known as the Review and Herald Publishing Association. She was the first single woman missionary of the Seventh-day Adventist Church, and she came with William Ings and his wife to join the small group in Switzerland. Maude and William both had been employees of the publishing house in Battle Creek and brought with them this helpful knowledge to add to the production, printing, and management of the publishing house that was started by this little group of Seventh-day Adventists.

It was great to have more hands to take up the mission work and also to be there to help with the daily chores of life. Mary did the best she could for a young girl with very little cooking experience, and they all found Mrs. Ings's recipes a welcome change.

Unfortunately, since arriving in Switzerland three years earlier, the Andrews family had been experiencing both exhaustion and a lack of nutrition. These things had already begun to take their toll. In the fall pf 1878 Charles experienced his second great loss, not even a year after the Ingses and Maude had come to offer support. This time it was his sister, Mary. She had been doing her best at the publishing office, but her breathing had become labored, and she tired easily. When John Andrews was summoned to attend the General Conference session in September in Battle Creek, Michigan, it was agreed that he should take Mary. Charles stayed in Switzerland, and his father took his sister to Battle Creek to see Dr. John Harvey Kellogg. The diagnosis: tuberculosis. It was a devastating blow to their family. Mary died in November 1878. Charles and John communicated by their only means, letters. In a letter written to his father in December 1878, Charles penned these words of hope:

"If she has fallen asleep, I know that she has got safely through, that she will have part in the first resurrection. It will be but a short time till then."

Charles and John stayed in Basel and did their best to keep the publishing work moving forward. During this time Charles became acquainted with Marie Ann Dietschy. Their relationship had started to grow into a romantic one, but soon another loss would come to Charles. Five years after the death of his sister, Mary, he lost his father, John. John's health had not been as good as it should have been, and during a good part of his last years he was confined to his bed. Just after turning 26, Charles became an orphan.

RETURN TO THE UNITED STATES

After John's death, fellow church members thought it would be good for Charles to return to the United States and strengthen his printing and bindery talents. Charles was not able to take all his furniture with him, so he left the pieces in the apartment so that they could be used by others. One of the first to make use of his bed, bureau, table, and wardrobe was Ellen White, when she came to stay at the publishing house there.

"Thank you for letting me leave a little early today. I want to be sure to meet Marie's train when it arrives. This will be her first time in the United States." The bindery foreman had to hide his smile. The excitement was pouring out of Charles, and who could blame him? The foreman could remember those days of young love between him and his wife. It was good to have something positive happening to the young man; he had already experienced so much loss.

Charles and Marie were married in 1886. The two welcomed three children: Harriet, John, and Edwin. Charles continued to work in the bindery and raise his family there in Battle Creek, Michigan. On December 30, 1902, there was a terrible fire, and the publishing house burned to the ground. Charles Andrews, like many other employees, was faced with the decision either to stay and find other work or to move to Washington, D.C., near Takoma Park, Maryland, where the new publishing house would be built. Charles and Marie decided to follow the publishing work they held dear.

In 1909 their oldest, Harriet, married the Review and Herald Publishing Association photographer, artist, and head of the art department, Sanford Harlan. Their son Russ became one of the most prolific painters of the Review and Herald (he is the artist who painted the picture of William Miller, shown on the first page of the Miller chapter).

Charles and Marie's son John, named after his grandfather, became a doctor and went on to follow in his grandfather's steps of missionary service.

July 19, 1915, was a very sad day for the Andrews family. The younger son, Edwin, at age 15, had come to the Review and Herald building in Takoma Park and was visiting his father and a family friend, editor Augustine Bourdeau, and his 10-year-old daughter, Marguerite. Church cofounder Ellen White had died three days earlier, on July 16, and on July 19, in Richmond, California, the second of three funerals for her was being held. Meanwhile, in Takoma Park the day was clear, so it was a great shock to hear a loud *CRACK* fill the air! Augustine, Edwin, and Marguerite went outside to examine the large oak tree that was near the Review and Herald and General Conference buildings.

CRACK! A second bolt of lightning split the air! Immediately Augustine and Edwin were killed. Marguerite was knocked unconscious with severe burns, leaving her with scars that she carried on her wrist until her death more than 70 years later.

Charles was a well-respected Review and Herald employee. It was voted that the company would cover the costs for the funeral and burials of Edwin and Augustine. What a tragic event!

A LIFE OF SERVICE FOR THE LORD

Charles's attention to detail and his care for quality printing and binding were always evident in his work. He was a dedicated worker for the Lord, binding Christ-centered books that can be found in homes all over the world!

When Charles died in 1927, his service was one of the most attended in Takoma Park, Maryland, at that time. His life is an example of hope and of keeping alive that hope and faith in Jesus, even when experiencing many personal losses and setbacks. Charles had hope in the return of the Lord and had a clear dedication to sharing the word of the Lord through the printed page!

THE HOPEFUL CHARLES ANDREWS

MARIE AND CHARLES ANDREWS

Mary Andrews

A Talented Young Woman

Mary followed her father, John Andrews, as he navigated the corridors of the S.S. *Atlas* to locate the room that they would occupy for the next few weeks. The ship had just begun to pull away from the port, and all the passengers on the deck had waved their final farewells to the well-wishers on land. The ship was abuzz with the activity of passengers and crew preparing for the journey. Mary made sure that she always kept her eyes on her father and her brother, Charles.

"This will be your bunk, and Charles will be in that one." Mary listened to her father, and then made her way over to the bunk so she could climb onto her bed, giving it a good test! "Let's go check on Mr. Vuilleumier. I believe his room isn't far from ours." Mary scrambled off the bed, excited and ready to start exploring the ship.

They quickly found their traveling companion, Adèmar Vuilleumier. Adèmar was heading home to Switzerland. He had been in the United States for two years. Now he would return with the Andrews family and assist them with translating and getting them settled in Switzerland.

The September breeze tugged at Mary's hair as she stood on the deck next to Charles. They could still see Boston, but that view would soon turn into an ocean. In two weeks she would be a teenager, just like Charles. She gave his hand a squeeze of nerves and excitement. What an adventure lay ahead!

THE PREACHER'S DAUGHTER

Mary Frances Andrews was born to John and Angeline Andrews on September 29, 1861, in Waukon, Iowa. Her older brother, Charles, turned 4 a few weeks after her birthday. The two spent much of her life together. By the time Mary was born, her father was a prominent writer, editor, speaker, and leader of the newly formed Seventh-day Adventist Church. This dedication often took him on work trips far from home. It wasn't long before the church members in New York, wanting to have John Andrews there more often, yet not wanting him to leave his young family, offered to financially assist in finding a home and moving them to Rochester, New York. With John still on the road, the move was made by Angeline with two little ones, Charles, 5, and Mary, not yet a year old. After this long absence from her father, little Mary didn't recognize him, and would fuss and cry when he tried to hold her. It broke John's heart and affirmed his need to be with his children. It didn't take long for Mary to become a "daddy's girl," settling into their new home in Rochester.

"Are you sure you are feeling up to it?" John's worried eyes searched Angeline's face. She had suffered a stroke weeks before, but today she was feeling better and wanted to go for a short walk. Ten-year-old Mary kept close to her mother's side as the family prepared for the outing. John helped Angeline into her coat. But the weight proved to be too much, and she collapsed to the ground. They didn't go for a walk that day, and Angeline, settled back in bed, died the next day. It was a tragic blow to both the children and their father.

Not long after her mother's death, the family, needing a change, moved to the city of South Lancaster, Massachusetts. There Mary and Charles had access to a good school and libraries. The two dove right into their studies.

A SWISS ADVENTURE

"I understand that there are many pressing needs, but I think we need to give special attention to the request from Switzerland."

"Yes, but I am not sure what more can be done." Mary often heard these conversations drifting around their house as church leaders came to visit with her father. So it did not come as a complete surprise to her when in 1874 her father announced that he had agreed to be the first missionary sent by the Seventh-day Adventist Church and that the two of them would be the first missionary children!

"When do we leave? Where will we live? Will people there understand me?" Mary peppered her father with questions. He smiled and pulled her into a gentle hug.

"I am not sure exactly when we will leave, but soon. We can stay with Mr. Vuilleumier and his family until we can find a place. I am not sure if anyone will be able to understand us, so we will need to start learning French as soon as we can." The young girl pushed back on his shoulders so she could see his face.

"Oui, mon père." Her accent needed some practice, and the three laughed at her attempt. It was good to hear their father laugh. He had been so sad since their mother's death.

Their missionary adventure didn't start in Switzerland. First, they stopped in England, Scotland, and France to visit and encourage small groups of believers. Now a 13-year-old, Mary spent a good part of the train rides across England and other European countries with her nose pressed against the window, watching the ever-changing landscapes!

Not long after arriving in Switzerland, the Andrewses found an apartment of their own. Mary took over the domestic duties, cooking as best she knew how, cleaning, and doing what she could to take their place a home.

ONLY ONE HOUR

"For only an hour?" Mary's eyes almost popped out of her head.

"Yes. We must learn these languages quickly." John was firm with his children. "We will reserve only one hour each day to speak English, and the rest of the time we will speak French or German."

Charles drew up a contract, and they all signed it. This way it would put some more emphasis on their decision.

"Then I tried to say a few words to the baker, but he didn't fully understand, so I think we have more loaves than I had wanted to buy." Mary took a deep breath. "After that, I was able to find a shortcut back to our place. What happened to you today?" Mary's words were coming at a machine-gun pace. Charles's speed matched her own.

"I found a new shop that sells butter at a lower price, and I was able to repair my shoes myself." The Andrewses lived on a very meager budget and carefully spent any money they had. The two exchanged a few more details of their day and talked about plans for tomorrow, but then the clock struck the hour, and just like that, their hour of English had ended.

Mary was a fast learner, and she was able to pick up French and German very well. John Andrews was a stickler for quality, especially when it came to the Lord's work. It didn't take long for him to note Mary's talent for editing, copy editing, and proofreading in both English and French! He would often write out the messages and articles in English, and then a new church member, Professor Louis Aufranc, would translate them into French. From there Mary would edit, copyedit, and proofread the copy. One day she received a high compliment from Professor Aufranc. He said, "Mary speaks French as though she were a French girl." Not yet 18, she had become a trusted and respected employee in the publishing work!

LONG WORKDAYS

The hours in the publishing office were long, and John, Charles, and Mary worked hard to reach as many readers as possible. It took a toll on their health, especially their father's. In January of 1877 John Andrews came to his children. He was trembling and had a deep pain in his right lung. Mary cast a worried look at Charles. This didn't look good, and he seemed so pale.

THE HOPEFUL **MARY ANDREWS**

Here they were in another country, far from home and from people they knew well. What to do?

"Father, I think we should call for a doctor," Mary said as she followed his request to pack him in hot, damp cloths. He emphatically declined. A doctor would cost precious dollars. Days passed, and Charles and Mary kept a close eye on their father, doing anything they could think of to ease his discomfort. When he didn't show signs of improvement, the children pushed him harder to allow the doctor to be called. He finally agreed.

Mary nervously let the doctor into the apartment and to her father's room. He went right to the patient to start his examination. She had been praying for her father's health since he first showed signs of sickness, and now she prayed an extra prayer for the doctor, asking that he may know how to heal their father.

"This man is almost starved to death!" The shocked words from the doctor broke into Mary's prayer. She knew that they were conservative with their food purchases, and often they ate only white bread. It was clear that his long work hours and lack of nutrient-filled food had contributed to his current illness. The doctor sat down with Charles and Mary and plainly gave them the diagnosis of pneumonia, and told them to prepare themselves for him not to survive. He promised to return soon and do what he could do.

Mary saw to her father's care. She turned all her focus on her father's health and what she could do. His health kept declining despite the doctor's efforts and the many, many prayers that she, Charles, and the Aufrancs could send. They sent a message about the bleak circumstances to Albert Vuilleumier, asking for him to pray. Albert arrived as soon as he received the message. He came into John Andrews' room and prayed, leaving the entire situation and John's health in God's hands. John was so sick he had no idea or memory of Albert's visit, but shortly after Albert left, his fever left him. It was the beginning of the miraculous healing process! His progress was slow, taking several weeks, but each day making a new step in the right direction.

MORE MISSIONARIES JOIN

Later that year Maude Sisley and William and Jenny Ings came to help the Andrewses and the Aufrancs with the publishing work in Switzerland. Mary welcomed them right away! It was so nice to have Jenny there to help with the cooking and household management. She saw how Maude and William were able to step right in and get the production part of their publishing work to produce a higher volume each day. It was an answer to prayer!

A DREADED DIAGNOSIS

As the weather started to turn cooler, Mary developed a cough. The cough turned worse and was accompanied by extreme tiredness. *You can do it. They need you to check the grammar for this issue; just one foot in front of the other,* Mary would say to herself each day, fighting the overwhelming fatigue and a cough that violently shook her thin frame.

"Please plan to attend the General Conference session taking place in Battle Creek." The words made John's heart do a little leap! He had to get Mary to Battle Creek with him. She was getting sicker and sicker, and he felt that if she could get to see Dr. John Harvey Kellogg in the Battle Creek Sanitarium, she might have a chance. Her illness and the request for Mary to accompany her father was presented to the church leaders, and arrangements were made for her to come to Battle Creek and see Dr. Kellogg. An answer to prayer!

The journey had less excitement than it had had four years ago. Her weak 16-year-old self didn't have the same interest as she had had the first time. And for the first time in her young life, she didn't have Charles close by. It felt so strange to be going so far away from him.

"Tuberculosis." The word hung in the air between them. Dr. Kellogg had just said it, and Mary couldn't lift her eyes from the blanket thread that she slowly twisted and untwisted around her finger. The doctors went to work right away to help her, but the disease had developed quite a bit, and her years of malnutrition didn't give her strong cells to rely on.

Mary celebrated her seventeenth birthday in the hospital. Her father never left her side, despite numerous warnings that the disease was contagious. Sadly, on November 27, 1878, Mary died from tuberculosis. John's loss was great. He had Mary's body shipped to Rochester so she could be buried beside her mother, Angeline.

A LIFE OF SERVICE

Mary Andrews loved the Lord and her family very much. She was steadfast and true in her work. She was hopeful and kept her eyes on Jesus even when things were sad, scary, or uncertain. Her young life was filled with courage and a willingness to be a missionary for the Lord!

Bibliography

Adventist Heritage 9, no. 1 (1984).

Bliss, Sylvester. *Memories of William Miller.* Leaves of Autumn Books. Reprint, 1988.

Burt, Merlin D. *Adventist Pioneer Places.* Hagerstown, Md.: Review and Herald Pub. Assn., 2011.

Byers, Carolyn. *Mary Andrews: Companion of Sorrows.* Washington, D.C.: Review and Herald Pub. Assn., 1983.

Chilson, Adriel D. *They Had a World to Win.* Hagerstown, Md.: Review and Herald Pub. Assn., 2001.

Coon, Roger. "Counsel to a Nervous Bridegroom." *Adventist Heritage* 13, no 2 (1990): 17-20.

Delafield, D. A. *Ellen G. White in Europe, 1885-1887.* Washington, D.C.: Review and Herald Pub. Assn., 1975.

Durand, Eugene. *Yours in the Blessed Hope.* Hagerstown, Md.: Review and Herald Pub. Assn., 1980.

Ellen G. White Estate document files.

General Conference of Seventh-day Adventists archives.

Gordon, P. A., and J. R. Nix. *Laughter and Tears of the Pioneers.* Teach Services, 1989.

Graybill, Ronald. "The Family Man." *Adventist Heritage* 9, no 1 (1984): 9-23.

Knight, George. *Joseph Bates.* Hagerstown, Md.: Review and Herald Pub. Assn., 2004

Maxwell, C. Mervyn. *Tell It to the World.* Mountain View, Calif.: Pacific Press Pub. Assn., 1977.

Nix, James R. *Early Advent Singing.* Hagerstown, Md.: Review and Herald Pub. Assn., 1994.

———. Oral presentation, May 29-June 1, 2001.

Pioneer Stories Retold. Washington, D.C.: Review and Herald Pub. Assn., 1956.

Robinson, Ella M. *Lighter of Gospel Fires.* Mountain View, Calif.: Pacific Press Pub. Assn., 1954.

Robinson, Virgil E. *Cabin Boy to Advent Crusader.* Nashville: Southern Pub. Assn., 1960.

———. *Flame for the Lord.* Washington, D.C.: Review and Herald Pub. Assn., 1975.

———. *James White.* Washington, D.C.: Review and Herald Pub. Assn., 1976.

Seventh-day Adventist Encyclopedia. Hagerstown, Md.: Review and Herald Pub. Assn., 1996.

Spalding, A. W. *Captains of the Host*. Washington, D.C.: Review and Herald Pub. Assn., 1949.

———. *Footprints of the Pioneers*. Washington, D.C.: Review and Herald Pub. Assn., 1947.

———. *Pioneer Stories. Nashville:* Southern Pub. Assn., 1922, 1942.

Spicer, W. A. *Pioneer Days*. Washington, D.C.: Review and Herald Pub. Assn., 1947.

Wheeler, Gerald. *James White*. Hagerstown, Md.: Review and Herald Pub. Assn., 2003.

White, Arthur L. *Ellen G. White*. Washington, D.C.: Review and Herald Pub. Assn., 1981-1986.

White, Ellen G. *Early Writings*. Washington, D.C.: Review and Herald Pub. Assn., 1882, 1945.

Zurcher, Jean. "The Christopher Columbus of Adventism." *Adventist Heritage* 9, no 1 (1984): 34-46.

Stories You'll Love

They look out at us from their portraits: earnest faces, still and sober for the photographer, above stiff collars and plain clothing. But who were they really, these strong-minded Adventist pioneers?

Learn more about the early pioneers:
They spent their lives, their health, their pennies, and their fortunes on spreading the three angels' message from the book of Revelation. In these two volumes you will find stories of the inspiring men and women who devoted their lives to knowing and sharing Biblical truths.

You Will See Your Lord a-Coming includes stories from the lives of:

- William and Lucy Miller
- Joseph and Prudy Bates
- Ellen and James White
- Hiram Edson
- Uriah and his sister Annie Smith
- and more!

Norma Collins spent her career researching and reading about these indivduals. Her words bring her discoveries to life and you will read stories that may be new to you. And gain a better understanding of the ups and downs in their lives, these stories inspiriing and continuing to share hope with each new generation.

Their Works Do Follow Them includes stories from the lives of:

- Maude Sisley Boyd
- Stephen and Hetty Haskell
- Anna Knight
- John Loughborough
- Stephen Smith
- and more!

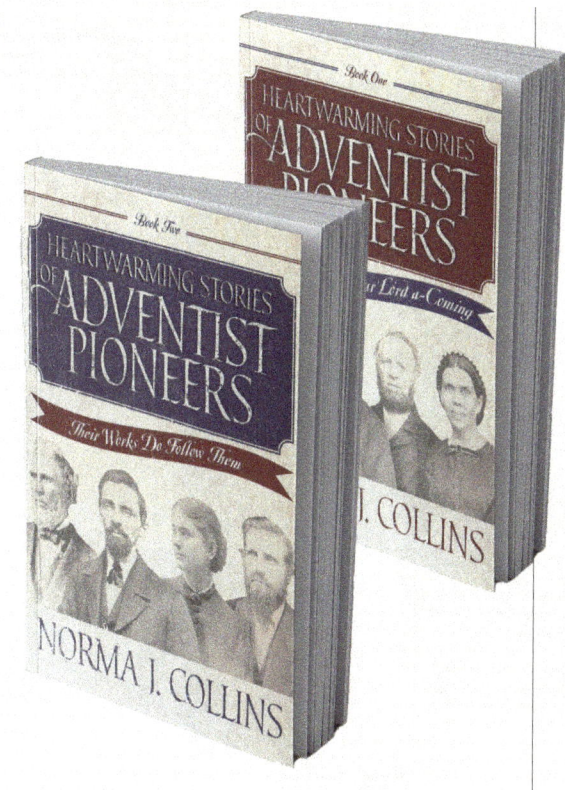

Scan for Volume One

Scan for Volume Two

SHOP YOUR WAY
» **Visit** your local Adventist Book Center
» **Call** toll-free 800.765.6955
» **Click** www.adventistbookcenter.com
» **Click** GooglePlay

Review & Herald

REVIEW AND HERALD® PUBLISHING ASSOCIATION | SINCE 1861 | WWW.REVIEWANDHERALD.COM

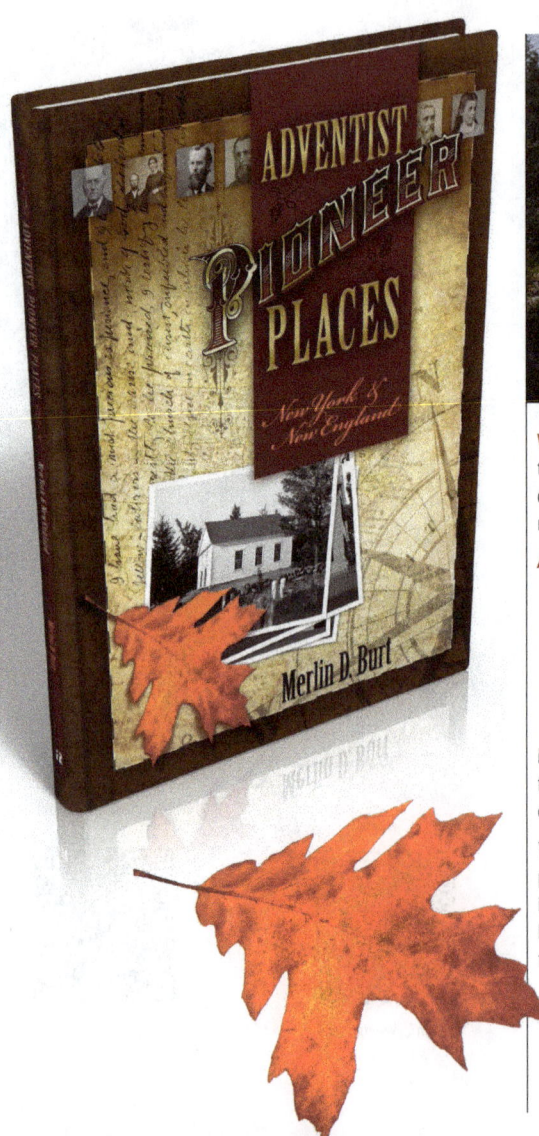

Take the Tour

Visit the sites where the Adventist faith began: the pioneers' homes and churches, the sites of births and deaths, the special places where visions descended and revival arose.

Adventist Pioneer Places includes:
- maps
- current, color photographs of landmarks
- historic photographs
- stories that illuminate the lives of the pioneers
- GPS coordinates

Merlin D. Burt's handbook serves as an invaluable guide for a trip in the family car or for a virtual tour taken in the comfort of your favorite reading chair.

You will feel inspired as you walk in the footsteps of people who, though weak and fallible, were used by God in remarkable ways to establish a global community of believers and begin a series of events that would eventually touch your own life.

Hardcover. 978-0-8280-2568-3

Hardcover   ebook

» **Visit** your local Adventist Book Center
» **Call** toll-free 800.765.6955
» **Click** www.adventistbookcenter.com
» **Click** GooglePlay

Review&Herald

REVIEW AND HERALD® PUBLISHING ASSOCIATION | SINCE 1861 | WWW.REVIEWANDHERALD.COM

www.ingramcontent.com/pod-product-compliance
Lightning Source LLC
Chambersburg PA
CBHW070156100426
42743CB00013B/2928